Praise for *Fearless Female Leaders*

"Empowering, insightful, and transformative! *Fearless Female Leaders* is the beacon for women's leadership. McAfee and Paetow masterfully chart the course to shatter glass ceilings. A must-read!"

~**Mayerland Harris**
Group VP of Talent, H-E-B

"I love this book! It provides me and other women with the path to finding confidence and the courage to overcome any barrier."

~**Jenna Barnett**
Inside Sales Manager, TTM Technologies / Aerospace & Defense

"A game-changer for women seeking to grow their confidence and truly understand and leverage the value they bring!"

~**Kelly Nygren**
Sales Leader, Global Toy Industry

"Learn from Kathy and Rosemary as you rise to the top of your world! Their experience and wisdom shared in this book will lighten the load and let you know you are not alone."

~**Dr. Dorothy Martin-Neville**
CEO of the Institute for Transformational Coaching and Leadership
Author of *Real Women Change the World*

"McAfee and Paetow are fearless voices extending their hands to light the path and claim our well-deserved seat at the leadership table."

~**Yolanda Canny**
Founder and Host, *Girl, Take the Lead!* podcast

"Jam-packed with stories that women will be able to relate to, see themselves in, and not feel alone. Applicable to women of all ages, *Fearless Female Leaders* guides young women toward becoming fearless leaders and more mature women to harness their own power."

~**Rowena Ortiz-Walters, PhD**
Dean and Professor of Management,
Greehey School of Business at St. Mary's University

"*Fearless Female Leaders* offers potent leadership growth tools that give women and men essential steps to become holistic, integrated humans in their leadership rather than 'half leaders' stuffed into rigid gender boxes that do all leaders (and humans) a disservice."

~**Kathy Caprino**
Author of *The Most Powerful You*
Career and Leadership Coach and Speaker
Senior Forbes Contributor

"This book is a gift for current and upcoming women leaders. It's filled with fearless stories of Sheroes and tools for success in work and life."

~**Wendy Green**
Host of the podcast *Hey Boomer!*
Certified Professional Coach, ACC

"This imperative guidebook deconstructs antiquated beliefs that have held women back from reaching their leadership potential, then creates a roadmap on how to get there."

~**Linda Nedell**
Founder and CEO of SAYge Link

"This book speaks to the power of perseverance. Emerging leaders taking on new roles—both women and men—will relish the insights from *Fearless Female Leaders*."

~**Marcia Daszko**
Consultant and Speaker
Author of *Pivot, Disrupt, Transform: How Leaders Beat the Odds and Survive*

"A lighthouse for navigating the Shero's Journey, illuminating the path to leadership with stories of women who've turned trials into triumphs."
~**Michele A. Wilson**
Host of the *Mompreneur Conversations*™ Network and Show
Advocate for mompreneurs raising special needs children

"A fascinating read with many great takeaways. A must-read for every woman who wants to break through the 'glass ceiling.'"
~**Dr. Larissa Winter**
Owner of Galagan ADVISORY
Founder of Purple Institute of Women

"Kathy and Rosemary are truly courageous leaders working tirelessly to develop and encourage women to become fearless leaders in today's challenging and changing work environment. Women are to get ready and be part of this change."
~**Maria Perdomo Arreaza**
European Senior Finance Manager, Securitas Technology

"This thought-provoking book is chock-full of relatable stories and useful resources for discovering your gifts and unleashing your potential. Read it for a compelling glimpse into your own story."
~**Rose Mihaly**
President, Mihaly Associates

"Women have always had the ability to be great leaders. It's the insecurities that often hold us back. This book gives us the tools and inspiration to step out of our shadows and shine."
~**Laura Biggerstaff**
Owner and CEO of Iron Elk, LLC

"The stories in *Fearless Female Leaders* inspire and touch the heart, while the strategies offer a wealth of pragmatic actions to develop and strengthen women leaders for the present and future."
~**Adrienne Milics**, MBA, PCC
Executive Coach

"McAfee and Paetow test our views of what defines leadership. With their inclusive leadership model, women can reach their untapped potential—authentically. It's time to lead."

~**Candace Freedenberg**
CEO and Founder of Untapped Potential, Inc.

"Such an inspirational read and must-have tool kit for those ready to tap into their leadership potential. This book serves as an important reminder to pay it forward by empowering other females to become fearless leaders."

~ **Jocelyn Belisle**
Retired, Chief Accounting Officer, Stanley Black & Decker, Inc.

FEARLESS
Female
LEADERS

STORIES AND STRATEGIES TO EMPOWER MORE WOMEN TO LEAD

Kathy McAfee & Rosemary Paetow

Foreword by Teresa C. Younger,
President & CEO of Ms. Foundation for Women

PYP Publish Your Purpose

Copyright © 2024 Kmc Brand Innovation, LLC. All rights reserved.

Fearless Female Leaders is part of the Fearless Leader Books™ series.

The Fearless Leader™, Fearless Leader Books™, and America's Marketing Motivator™ are pending trademarks of Kmc Brand Innovation, LLC.

No part of this publication shall be reproduced, transmitted, or sold in whole or in part in any form without prior written consent of the author, except as provided by the United States of America copyright law. Any unauthorized usage of the text without express written permission of the publisher is a violation of the author's copyright and is illegal and punishable by law. All trademarks and registered trademarks appearing in this guide are the property of their respective owners.

For permission requests, write to the publisher, addressed "Attention: Permissions Coordinator," at the address below.

Publish Your Purpose
141 Weston Street, #155
Hartford, CT, 06141

PYP Publish Your Purpose

The opinions expressed by the author are not necessarily those held by Publish Your Purpose.

Ordering Information: Quantity sales and special discounts are available on quantity purchases by corporations, associations, and others. For details, contact the publisher at hello@publishyourpurpose.com.

For more information about The Fearless Leader™ programs, Fearless Leader Books™ series, speaking engagements or media interviews, please contact Kathy McAfee at Kathy@TheFearlessLeader.com or visit www.TheFearlessLeader.com.

Edited by Nancy Graham-Tillman, Lily Capstick, and Hermine Fuerst Garcia
Cover design by: Julia Kuris
Illustrations by: Megan L. Robinson

ISBN: 979-8-88797-094-3 (hardcover)
ISBN: 979-8-88797-095-0 (paperback)
ISBN: 979-8-88797-096-7 (ebook)

Library of Congress Control Number: 2023922382

First Edition, June 2024.

The information contained within this book is strictly for informational purposes. The material may include information, products, or services by third parties. As such, the author and publisher do not assume responsibility or liability for any third-party material or opinions. The publisher is not responsible for websites (or their content) that are not owned by the publisher. Readers are advised to do their own due diligence when it comes to making decisions.

Publish Your Purpose is a hybrid publisher of nonfiction books. Our mission is to elevate the voices often excluded from traditional publishing. We intentionally seek out authors and storytellers with diverse backgrounds, life experiences, and unique perspectives to publish books that will make an impact in the world. Do you have a book idea you would like us to consider publishing? Please visit PublishYourPurpose.com for more information.

To cite this work (Chicago style): McAfee, Kathy, and Rosemary Paetow. *Fearless Female Leaders: Stories and Strategies to Empower More Women to Lead*. Hartford, CT: Publish Your Purpose, 2024.

Dedication

To Nancy Sheffield (1961–2022), my lifelong friend. You were the most fearless female I have ever known. I will remember you always.

~Kathy

To my mother and father, Maria (1934–1999) and Herbert von Hammerstein (1932–1993). Mom, you were and still are my rock of Gibraltar, and Dad, you gave me all the tools to be a leader.

~Rosemary

Table of Contents

Dedication   ix
Foreword   xv
A Tale of Two Leaders Illustrated   xviii
How We Got Here in the First Place   xix

PART 1: A COSTLY PROBLEM:
Overlooking Women's Leadership Potential   1

1   **Survey Says, Going Nowhere Fast**   3
    Barriers to Leadership Advancement for Women   7
    Five Years Ago (2017–2021)   7
    Last Twelve Months (2021–2022)   10
    Four Big Takeaways   12

2   **Leadership Origin Stories: Recognizing Our Gifts**   13
    Kathy McAfee
    From Songleader to Creative Entrepreneur   14
    Rosemary Paetow
    From Tennis Champion to Champion of Leaders   19

3   **Owning Your Leadership Potential**   25
    Your Leadership Origins   26
    Your Conscious and Unconscious Limiting Beliefs   28
    Uncovering Your Leadership Shadow   29
    Making Peace with Your Leadership Shadow   31
    Creating Your Fearless Leader Manifesto   33

PART 2: INSPIRED SOLUTIONS:
Owning Your Story & Becoming More Fearless — **43**

4   **Embodying Attributes of Fearless Leadership**   **45**
- Attribute #1: Boldness — 47
- Attribute #2: Intuition — 48
- Attribute #3: Compassion — 50
- Attribute #4: Confidence — 53
- Attribute #5: Resonance — 55
- Attribute #6: Resilience — 56
- Attribute #7: Wisdom — 58
- Attribute #8: Humor — 60
- What's Next? — 62

5   **Reinventing Leadership / Resolving Problems**   **63**
- Problem #1: Not Having a Mentor — 64
- Problem #2: No Flexibility at Work or Support at Home — 69
- Problem #3: Lack of Confidence — 72
- Problem #4: Ageism — 74
- Changing the Journey — 76
- The Shero's Journey Illustrated — 77

PART 3: EMPOWERING ROLE MODELS:
Following Fearless Footsteps — **81**

6   **Focusing on What's Most Important**   **83**
- Sylvia Whitlock
  Fearless in the Face of Discrimination — 83
- Jane (Ballard) Dyer
  Fearless in the Face of Sexism — 87
- Valuable Lessons Learned — 91

7   **Developing Success Teams**   **93**
- Ms. Opal Lee
  The Fearless Face of Freedom — 94
- Eva Hausman
  Fearless in the Face of Indifference — 101
- Valuable Lessons Learned — 106

8	**Trusting That Our Gifts Are Wanted & Needed**	**109**
	Paula Stone Williams	
	The Fearless Face of Authenticity	110
	Kim Dechaine	
	Fearless in the Face of Depression	115
	Valuable Lessons Learned	120
9	**Creating New Ways to Lead**	**121**
	Jolly Lux	
	The Fearless Face of Resilience	121
	Wendy Fong	
	Fearless in the Face of the Old Boys' Club	127
	Valuable Lessons Learned	132
10	**Changing Everything**	**135**
	Channeling Your Inner Fearless Leader	137
	Fearlessly Changing Society	138
	Fearlessly Changing Workplace Infrastructure	140
	Stepping into Your Fearless Future	141

Appendix: Survey	145
Study Guide	149
More Fearless Resources	151
Bibliography	159
Acknowledgments	165
About the Authors	171

Foreword

In today's world, women are an undeniable force. They are on the cusp of leadership in a variety of fields, a potential that has been undervalued for too long. As a passionate advocate for gender equality and a leader with over three decades of executive-level experience, I wholeheartedly endorse the message of this book. As a former Girl Scout, instilled with a lifelong mission to make the world a better place, I'm here to tell you that the time for women's leadership has come, and this book is your guide to unleash it.

Stepping into my role as President and CEO of the Ms. Foundation for Women, I embraced the mission to build women's collective power to advance equity and justice for all. We invested in and strengthened the capacity of women-led movements to advance social, cultural, and economic change in the lives of women and society. These movements embody the essence of fearless female leadership, and they are driven by an unshakable commitment to create a better world. These leaders understand that women's leadership must encompass bravery, boldness, humor, and joy.

Having traveled extensively across the United States and around the globe, I've had the privilege of meeting some of the most wonderful, strong, creative, and compassionate women leaders. Their stories have fueled my conviction that the world is teeming with untapped potential and that this potential is intrinsically tied to their desire and mission to improve the world and the unique lived experiences they bring to the work they do. The women we encounter within the pages of this book are no exception, and their journeys are a testament to the power of fearless female leadership, enriched by these qualities.

Women continue to face both external and internal barriers that relegate them to the shadows of leadership. The mentorship, flexibility, and support necessary to ascend to their rightful place as leaders have been in short supply. But the journey you are about to embark upon introduces you to a select group of remarkable women who have confronted these barriers head-on, emerging as fearless leaders with an unshakable desire to create positive change in the world. They possess the bravery to challenge the status quo, the boldness to disrupt norms, and the wisdom to infuse humor and joy into their leadership.

Authors McAfee and Paetow, with their extensive knowledge and experience, provide readers with the tools and guidance they need to transform their perspectives. Through their exploration of eight great attributes of fearless leadership, a fusion of both masculine and feminine leadership styles, they offer a clear path to success and personal fulfillment, all anchored in the belief that women's leadership must encompass bravery, boldness, and humor.

As a champion of movements for gender equity and justice, I can attest to the profound significance of gender equality in leadership. It's not merely a moral imperative; it's an absolute necessity. The world, especially the business world, stands to benefit immeasurably from increased female representation in leadership roles. This book peels back the layers of self-doubt and societal constraints, offering a roadmap for women to break free from convention and discover the fearless leader within.

The stories you are about to read are more than just accounts of adversity and triumph; they are testimonies to courage, tenacity, and grace. They are a living testament to the fact that women can rise above daunting challenges to lead with unwavering determination, and they do so with a sense of purpose and delight that inspires those around them.

So, as you embark on this journey through the narratives of remarkable women, seize this opportunity to embrace your own fearless leadership potential. Become inspired by their movements in striving for equity and justice. I encourage you to unleash your voice, your

FOREWORD

vision, and your strength, and to take the world by storm. Together, we will transcend the barriers that have held us back and emerge as the leaders we were always meant to be. The transformation begins now!

Teresa C. Younger
President and CEO of Ms. Foundation for Women

Illustration by Megan L. Robinson

How We Got Here in the First Place

I am woman, hear me roar / In numbers too big to ignore.
~Helen Reddy, 1972

This book is about female leadership—the barriers and fears, and the untold opportunities that await us individually and collectively when we allow women and girls to step into their greatness and realize their full leadership potential in all facets of society.

According to psychologist and bestselling author Daniel Goleman, two of the most important leadership attributes are connection and emotion. And we believe that women are biologically wired and gifted to lead in this way. In his book *Primal Leadership*, coauthored by Annie McKee and Richard E. Boyatzis, Goleman concludes that great leadership works through emotions. Even if a leader gets everything else right, if they don't drive emotions in the right direction, nothing they do will work as well as it could or should.[1] Emotional intelligence, then, and the ability to positively direct emotion, are critical abilities for a leader.

So why are women in the workforce constantly told to leave their emotions at home? Why has there been so much resistance to female

---

[1] Daniel Goleman, Annie McKee, and Richard E. Boyatzis, *Primal Leadership: Realizing the Power of Emotional Intelligence* (Boston: Harvard Business School Press 2002), 3.

leadership? More importantly, if women are "natural leaders," then why aren't they beating down the doors of executive suites? Why is it that only 15 percent of CEO positions in Fortune 500 publicly traded companies are held by women?[2] Why are only 41 of the current S&P 500 companies led by women?[3]

To answer these questions, we need to explore what's in the way of female leadership, why it's so important to change this paradigm, and how to begin the "change process" without the typical method for radical change: a revolution. We propose a more peaceful path to fearless change.

Women have already had two revolutions in their attempt to claim their leadership place in American society: once in the 1920s when they claimed their voices with the right to vote, and a second in the 1960s when they were finally recognized for their contributions by securing equal pay for equal work. Yet women still aren't commanding the key leadership roles in Corporate America. In fact, we're seeing an alarming trend that many top female leaders, especially in the technology industry, are leaving and not being replaced.

Origins of Leadership

To understand what's happening, we first need to look at the origin of how leaders come into being. Back in the day (several thousand years ago), the leadership mantle was handed to two kinds of people: those born into it (rulers and nobility) and those who earned it (heroes, members of the military, and financiers). Today, though many people with monetary status are still automatically given the mantle of leadership, new opportunities are now opening for those who earn that role irrespective of caste, status, or birth. If we look at how these opportunities

---

[2] Katharina Buchholz, "How Has the Number of Female CEOs in Fortune 500 Companies Changed over the Last 20 Years?" World Economic Forum, March 10, 2022, https://www.weforum.org/agenda/2022/03/ceos-fortune-500-companies-female.

[3] "Women CEO's in America" 2022 Annual Report by Women Business Collaborative (WBC), with Ascend, C200 and Catalyst. https://wbcollaborative.org/women-ceo-report/the-report/2023-executive-summary/.

arise, we can see that more potential leaders are being identified and trained. What can we do to include more women in the creation of these opportunities?

Historical Leadership Training

Consider that leaders who *earn* a spot in leadership rather than being handed the job due to winning the "birth lottery" do so today because of training and on-the-job experience. And that begins with defining the qualities of a leader. Traditionally, men have defined those qualities through two avenues: the stories they tell and the games they play. All those little league games serve as vehicles for teaching little boys how to lead, how to follow, and how to be part of a team. At an early age, this training separates the ones who want to lead from those who want to follow. Leading must be experienced, and team sports provide a safe and fun way to gain that experience. They also model the tools that effective leaders need:

- A goal or objective (to win the game)
- A good advisor (the coach) to lay out the strategy
- Followers who can execute the plan (teammates)
- A leadership pool from which they can identify potential candidates (teammates)

So, young boys who play sports are taught the art and science of leadership for some fifteen to twenty years before they enter the workforce. They are primed and ready to be part of a team and become leaders. That's quite the advantage. Up until recently, it's one that hasn't been fully accessible to women.

When women entered the workforce in the 1940s, they didn't have the same leadership training that men had. Unlike that of men, women's leadership training involved managing resources and relationships. As mothers, they had to work within a budget and make sure that their family dynamics produced the right environment for goal achievement. In the case of being a mom, this meant creating an environment that supported the leader of the family—the husband—by providing stability so that he could go off and bring home the bacon, so to speak. Moms are the classic example of supportive leaders.

When women entered the workplace, they weren't rewarded for knowing how to be supportive leaders. They were given lower-level jobs and paid less. Something needed to change to level the playing field. So in the 1960s, women had their second revolution to declare their right to equal pay and equal status. This particular revolution helped raise awareness and transparency, but the wage gap for women in the workforce continues to be an ongoing issue, especially for women of color.

In 1973, *Roe v. Wade* passed, giving women the right and power to choose when or if they had children. In 1975, little girls in the United States were allowed to start playing in little league team sports. And just like that, little girls started to experience masculine leadership training in the same way that boys do. By the early 2000s, they were kicking ass in Corporate America. Evidently, the two biggest factors in women's managerial success were having control over their bodies and being trained to lead.

Then, in 2019, women hit another big milestone: they surpassed the 50 percent mark within the US workforce.[4] That same year, women occupied 50.8 percent of all management, professional, and other leadership-related occupations.[5] These gains, however, were soon put to the challenge in the form of a global pandemic. With all nonessential businesses and most schools closed, women with young children were called to take on additional leadership responsibilities at home, including being full-time teachers and afterschool activities directors. As a result, millions of women left the workforce, not to return.

---

[4] Richard Fry, "U.S. Women Near Milestone in the College-Educated Labor Force," Pew Research Center, June 20, 2019, https://www.pewresearch.org/short-reads/2019/06/20/u-s-women-near-milestone-in-the-college-educated-labor-force/.

[5] "Labor Force Statistics from the Current Population Survey," U.S. Bureau of Labor Statistics, accessed October 4, 2023, https://www.bls.gov/cps/aa2019/cpsaat10.htm.

Reversing Currents

The hard gains made by women in management and leadership were quickly erased by the COVID-19 global pandemic. The recovery was slow, and regaining lost ground proved to take much longer than anyone expected. Then came the next major blow to the future of women's leadership potential. In 2022, *Roe v. Wade*, the Supreme Court case that made abortion a nationally protected civil right for women for almost fifty years, was overturned. This is a direct assault on women's civil rights and women's health, and it has created more barriers to women participating in the workforce and advancing in leadership. No matter what your personal view on abortion is, there's no debating the negative impact this nullification will have on women's professional careers and earning potential.

The "motherhood penalty" epitomizes such reversing currents. Coined by sociologists, the term describes the discrimination working mothers experience in the workplace compared with their female counterparts without children and men regardless of parental status.[6] According to psychotherapist and research consultant Dr. Rachel Diamond, society penalizes working moms for having kids and rewards fathers. In an article in *Psychology Today*, she identified three issues that impact working mothers:

1. Being perceived as less competent and less committed
2. Having fewer professional development opportunities
3. Receiving less pay[7]

Additional research conducted by Michelle J. Budig, a professor at the University of Massachusetts Amherst, suggests that a woman's earning power drops by 4 percent for every child she has. Men, on

---

[6] "The Motherhood Penalty," American Association of University Women, accessed October 4, 2023, https://www.aauw.org/issues/equity/motherhood/.

[7] Rachel Diamond, "The Motherhood Penalty in the Workplace," Psychology Today, February 13, 2023, https://www.psychologytoday.com/us/blog/preparing-for-parenthood/202302/the-motherhood-penalty-in-the-workplace#:~:text.

the other hand, have a different experience, with fathers receiving greater opportunities and increased wages. "Fatherhood is seen as a valued characteristic by employers, signaling perhaps greater work commitment, stability, and deservingness."[8] On the other hand, employers view mothers as unreliable due to the "distraction" of family responsibilities.

The impact of these sociological biases combined with the increasing restrictions on women's reproductive freedom poses a serious threat to women in the workforce, one that could result in even fewer women in the eligible leadership pool. This is a reason we need women in top leadership and decision-making positions. We need them to fight for the flexibility and protection that working mothers and families need.

Something needs to change. Now. We think it starts by defining what it means to be a leader, followed by training and developing more emerging female leaders within a larger leadership talent pool to lead as women.

Defining "Leader"

Our definitions of leadership are embedded in the stories we tell. Our movies and news outlets are filled with what society says good leaders are. These days, in their desire to appeal to a bigger audience and become more inclusive, directors and producers cast a Black hero, a Hispanic hero, an Asian hero, a female hero, or an LGBTQ+ hero, but they are all still modeled after male heroes. The defining attributes of leadership are still masculine characteristics, such as grit, boldness, confidence, and competitiveness. We think that needs to change for society to flourish.

Companies that have leadership diversity make more money, last longer, and grow bigger, so it's in all of our best interests to incorporate

---

[8] Michelle J. Budig, "The Fatherhood Bonus and The Motherhood Penalty: Parenthood and the Gender Gap in Pay," Third Way, September 2, 2014, https://www.thirdway.org/report/the-fatherhood-bonus-and-the-motherhood-penalty-parenthood-and-the-gender-gap-in-pay.

diversity into leadership. To do that, our storylines must change from those of a hero's journey to those of a heroine's journey.

The Hero's Journey

According to American mythologist and writer Joseph Campbell, who popularized the concept of a hero's journey, the hero needs to fulfill three basic steps:

- A call to action that separates them from their community or the status quo in order to solve a problem
- A crisis of identity while resolving the problem through a series of trials that excise their limiting beliefs
- A transformation that ultimately integrates male leadership attributes and defines them as a powerful leader[9]

The existing hero's journey typically involves him returning as a victor and assuming the leadership mantle after he has learned the skills needed to succeed and transform his relationship with failure. And he, like all successful heroes before him, needs to learn to use failure as a learning tool. It's what makes him a winner, champion, and celebrated leader. The heroine's journey is a bit different. It involves a rejection of her feminine qualities in favor of embodying the masculine characteristics of power and control.

The Heroine's Journey

After interviewing Joseph Campbell in 1981 and becoming very dissatisfied with his view that women don't need to make a hero's journey, Maureen Murdock, a Jungian psychotherapist, spent eight years researching and publishing her own influential book called *The Heroine's Journey*. It has been in print for more than thirty years and

---

[9] Joseph Campbell, *The Hero with a Thousand Faces* (New Jersey: Princeton University Press, 2004), 45–233.

expands on the hero's journey storyline to specifically include women. In summary, the heroine's journey looks like this:

1. A call for power and control
2. Rejecting her feminine ideals
3. Embracing external masculine ideals or values
4. A crisis of wholeness / trials of integration
5. Embodying masculine values (external empowerment)
6. Reconnecting with her feminine values (internal empowerment)
7. An emergence of a balanced, holistic leadership approach[10]

Murdock notes that the point of the heroine's journey is to integrate her feminine values with masculine ones, which creates a leadership expression that includes the whole woman. Most movies that have a female hero, however, show her rejecting her feminine ideals to embrace the masculine ones that promote power and kicking some ass. End of story. But that stops short of the full heroine's journey. She's supposed to take the next step of integrating and balancing the masculine and feminine leader characteristics, the way they do in *Moana*, *Coraline*, *Madeline*, and *The Woman King*. Most other movies don't give women the full picture of feminine leadership. They show a woman how to be a male hero. And male sports training doubles down on that.

The Shero's Journey

As female leaders ourselves, we suggest a variation on the hero's and heroine's journeys: moving from two separate processes that men and women individually experience toward an integrated, holistic process that they both participate in and results in the same outcome—a cohesive leader. This approach gives both men and women the opportunity to be holistic, or whole leaders rather than half leaders (either masculine *or* feminine).

---

[10] Maureen Murdock, *The Heroine's Journey: Woman's Quest for Wholeness* (Boulder, CO: Shambhala, 2020), 5.

HOW WE GOT HERE IN THE FIRST PLACE

We've chosen the word "Shero" to describe this new inclusive leadership model. Though standard dictionaries describe the word "hero" as a person who is admired or idealized for their courage, outstanding achievements, or noble qualities, history has defined the term to include only men. For our purposes, we'd like to change the noun to Shero to be inclusive of *all* people and *all* leaders, regardless of gender or identity.

In our new model, the "Shero's Journey," the storyline looks like this:

1. A call to action (some change is required)
2. A series of trials
3. Identify the masculine attributes needed to lead
4. Identify the female qualities needed to balance masculine values
5. Identify and eliminate limiting beliefs
6. Holistic integration (combine masculine and feminine leadership attributes)
7. Development (choose the desired leadership potential and path to fulfill, after which transformation occurs)

Let the journey begin.

PART 1

A COSTLY PROBLEM:

Overlooking Women's Leadership Potential

CHAPTER 1

Survey Says, Going Nowhere Fast

No country can ever truly flourish if it stifles the potential of its women and deprives itself of the contributions of half of its citizens.
~Michelle Obama

Before we unleash the powerful new you into the world, we must first examine the barriers to leadership advancement that women still face today. To bring you up to speed on the progress made over the last five years, as well as the roadblocks that continue to hinder women in the workplace, we'll share the results from our proprietary research and what they might mean to you and the professional women in your organization.

Some may argue that women have already broken through the "glass ceiling." Over the last fifty years, women have made great strides economically and socially. According to Pew Research Center, women now earn 82 percent of what men make in the same role with the same qualifications (up from 80 percent in 2002).[11] In addition, unmarried

---

[11] Rakesh Kochhar, "The Enduring Grip of the Gender Pay Gap," Pew Research Center, March 1, 2023, https://www.pewresearch.org/social-trends/2023/03/01/the-enduring-grip-of-the-gender-pay-gap/.

women can now buy real estate without a male cosigner, and married women now have credit established when they divorce.[12] Best of all, women have captured 15 percent of all CEO roles in American publicly traded companies.[13]

But is this good enough? Do we stand a fighting chance of succeeding, or is the deck stacked against us? Are these statistics representative of our talent and our capacity? At the current rate of advancement, it will take 450 years to reach parity. Can we wait that long? Can the world afford to wait that long?

Equally important to consider is that many of these executive women have been elevated to lead during problematic times and offered precarious positions when the risk of failure is high, a phenomenon known as the "glass cliff."[14] Even with the high chance of failure, a glass cliff position can be difficult for a woman to turn down because leadership roles are so infrequently offered to them.

The reality is that women continue to be overlooked and undervalued in accessing the pool of future leaders. Also, their experience at home isn't counted as legitimate work; currently it isn't captured in global domestic product figures by any country. But if it were measured, women's unpaid labor would be worth almost $11 trillion globally, according to a 2019 *New York Times* article: "If American women earned minimum wage for the unpaid work they do around the house and caring for relatives, they would have earned $1.5 trillion last year."[15] That exceeds the combined revenue of the fifty largest companies on the 2019 Fortune Global 500 list, including Walmart, Apple, and Amazon. Indeed, women produce more economic value than they are given credit for.

---

[12] "Equal Credit Opportunity Act," Federal Trade Commission, accessed October 4, 2023, https://www.ftc.gov/legal-library/browse/statutes/equal-credit-opportunity-act.
[13] Buchholz, "the Number of Female CEOs."
[14] Julia Kagan, "Glass Cliff: Definition, Research, Examples, vs. Glass Ceiling," Investopedia, last modified December 7, 2022, https://www.investopedia.com/terms/g/glass-cliff.asp#.
[15] Gus Wezerek and Kristen R. Ghodsee, "Women's Unpaid Labor is Worth $10,900,000,000," *New York Times*, March 5, 2020, https://www.nytimes.com/interactive/2020/03/04/opinion/women-unpaid-labor.html.

We know intrinsically that the value women produce at home, even if they aren't being compensated for it, is priceless. But what's hard to understand is why many women are stigmatized at work for their dual responsibilities. The frustrations can be maddening for many women with leadership ambitions, as Amanda's story conveys.

A Glimpse

Amanda has worked for a company for seven years and is one of its top sales producers. Her scores for client relationship management are off the charts, and she's a team player. Prior to the pandemic, Amanda spent 50 percent of her work time traveling because it was part of the job that she enjoyed. With the support of her husband, they managed their kids' schedules. So when Amanda applied for the job of director of client management, she was surprised that they didn't choose her. They hired a man outside the company, and he turned out to be an "old-school thinking" kind of leader.

Things progressively became more difficult for Amanda under his management. He didn't see her value or her potential, and he wasn't interested in developing her skills or advancing her career at the company. Amanda's frustration and disappointment continued to fester under his leadership. But she loved the company and was holding out hope for a promotion despite him—that is until the day she sat down with him to ask why he chose someone else and not her for the recent role she interviewed for.

Without realizing he was breaking company policy, he said, "I assumed you wouldn't be able to do this job, as it requires lots of travel. And with two kids, how in the world would you manage the travel demands of this new position? Better that you stay in your current position."

Not willing to let this go, but needing to be professional and diplomatic, Amanda went to her divisional leader (we'll call her Pamela) to gain more perspective on these recent hiring decisions. She also needed to know whether there was a future for her at this company or was it time to find opportunities outside the company. Here's how the exchange went:

Amanda: "I noticed that we've been hiring a lot of people from outside the organization. Why is that?"
Pamela: "Well, we really need to ratchet up our sales numbers. And we need new energy and new leadership."
Amanda: "How's it been going so far?"
Pamela: "Of course, we expected a lag before a new leader can get up to speed."
Amanda: "You may not realize that I have been the top sales performer on this team for the past five years. My numbers grew even during the pandemic. Did you not consider promoting me—a proven performer—into this leadership spot?"
Pamela: "We did consider you, but we felt you weren't quite ready. We needed more leadership experience for this important role."

Passed up. Placated. Put down.
Is this how we want to treat our top performers?

Amanda's experience is not uncommon. The leadership gender gap remains significant, persistent, and systemic even though statistically companies that have women in key leadership roles perform better, are more profitable, and last longer[16] Better run, more profitable companies translate into more stable economies, and we could all use more stability and more money in our pockets. Obviously the business world could benefit from having more women in leadership roles, so why is

---

[16] Corinne Post and Chris Byron, "Women on Boards and Firm Financial Performance: A Meta-Analysis," Academy of Management Journal 58, no. 5 (October 2015), https://journals.aom.org/doi/10.5465/amj.2013.0319.

female leadership happening so slowly? Why do women continue to be the underdogs of the working world? What are the barriers to women's leadership advancement, and how can women overcome them?

Barriers to Leadership Advancement for Women

To answer these questions and ground ourselves in what women experience beyond our own personal stories, we decided to conduct a survey in the winter of 2022–2023.[17] You can view a copy of our survey by scanning the QR code found in the appendix of this book. We wanted to hear what women saw was in the way of their successful transition into a leadership role. Based on our readings and personal experiences, we compiled a list of sixteen gender-based barriers to include in the survey and asked respondents to mark which ones they were facing in their careers. We then asked respondents to rank in order their top three barriers and describe them in their own words.

In analyzing the survey responses, we thought it would be beneficial to capture the answers by age category to determine whether age impacts such experiences. To see whether we have made any real strides, we also asked participants to evaluate what it was like five years prior to the survey and what it has been like during the most recent twelve-month period.

Five Years Ago (2017–2021)

The women cited three primary reasons their career progress had been hindered between early 2017 and late 2021:

1. Being female
2. A lack of flexibility in the work environment
3. Women sabotaging women

---

[17] In total, we collected 121 survey responses between November 4, 2022, and February 24, 2023.

The good news is that, according to these women's self-assessments, these three particular barriers started to break down during this five-year period and some inroads to accepting women into management ranks were made. It seems that simply being female is no longer a deterrent in becoming a manager. We think this shift may be related to the #MeToo movement, which among other things put a spotlight on conscious and unconscious biases toward promoting females. The movement also had women realizing the importance of supporting other women in the workplace as they began to see how prevalent prejudice and harassment were. Many workplaces began to realize the value of having women in management roles.

Statistically, companies that have women managers have higher profits,[18] and studies show that "Countries with school-age girls who score highly on math tests were more likely to have women in management positions . . . The larger the pool, the more you're going to see make it to that very top level."[19] These are great data points for making a business case for why women should be proactively developed across the leadership pipeline. If companies want to ensure a prosperous future, they need to get more creative and progressive in how they attract, retain, and leverage women talent in their workforces. And if they want more women in their management ranks, companies will have to become more flexible with when women start and end their days. Flexibility could be the magic strategy to drive increased profits.

---

[18] Marcus Noland and Tyler Moran, "Study: Firms with More Women in the C-Suite Are More Profitable," Peterson Institute for International Economics, February 8. 2016, https://www.piie.com/commentary/op-eds/study-firms-more-women-c-suite-are-more-profitable.

[19] Daniel Victor, "Women in Company Leadership Tied to Stronger Profits, Study Says," New York Times, February 9, 2016, https://www.nytimes.com/2016/02/10/business/women-in-company-leadership-tied-to-stronger-profits.html.

A Glimpse

When coauthor Rosemary was an auditor at KPMG in 1990, a senior manager approached her and asked why the company wasn't retaining its female staff. By the time they were eligible to be promoted to management positions (company policy required four years of service), only 20 percent of them were still working at the firm.

Her manager walked her through the math: "Look. If we hire ten women, by the time they are eligible to become a manager there will be only two of them left. This is an abnormal attrition rate. Why is this happening?"

The answer was obvious to Rosemary. She responded matter-of-factly, "There's no flexibility for women to have babies, work around daycare hours, or take time off to attend their children's activities. You force them to choose between work and their families. What would you do?"

This short conversation was an aha moment for Rosemary's manager. His eyes opened to what he himself had never experienced and didn't understand. When he shared this new insight with his executive team, KPMG leaders realized that if they didn't change their business practices, they'd continue to lose some of their best talent at extraordinary rates. They added benefits such as flex-scheduling and maternity leave without loss of stature, which was good not only for morale but for retaining top talent.

These days, most public accounting firms (or at least the innovative ones) have flexibility around work times. They've learned to keep their top talent by changing their business models. But not all industries are as advanced. Flex time is still an unresolved issue in many companies. When the pandemic hit, most companies had to incorporate flex time. Now that the crisis is over, many want to go back to the old way of having everyone work from the office at set times. But most employees, including men, have come to realize the benefits of working from home. They're more productive, and their family lives are better. Men are now demanding what women have been requesting for years: greater flexibility so that a better work–life balance can be achieved and enjoyed by all.

Are you curious how the women who eventually left KPMG—and coincidentally were the top 10 percent of their graduating class—accomplished their professional and personal goals? They started their own businesses. They became tax accountants, consultants, and accounting specialists. Some even started companies in other fields as well.

Last Twelve Months (2021–2022)

Turning toward changes since 2021, our survey identified four primary factors that had been getting in the way of women's leadership advancement over the most recent twelve-month period (irrespective of age bracket):

1. Not having a mentor
2. No flexibility at work or support at home
3. Lack of confidence
4. Ageism

It's interesting to note that while survey respondents indicated that flexibility has vastly improved in the last five years, the issue remains problematic for women in their thirties, forties, fifties, and sixties. From an age perspective, the reasons that slow leadership progress for these women are as follows:

- Thirties—a lack of flexibility in the work environment, limited support at home, lack of mentorship, and women sabotaging women
- Forties—a lack of mentorship, confidence, flexibility, and support
- Fifties—a lack of mentorship, flexibility and support; ageism
- Sixties and beyond—a lack of mentorship and confidence; ageism

In part 2 of this book, we'll look at how to solve these problems. In part 3 of this book we'll hear from some very inspiring women who've overcome these barriers in some extraordinary ways. They are ordinary women becoming fearless leaders. Their journeys haven't been easy, but they are noble. Like us, the coauthors, these women have had to face their fears and change some limiting beliefs that were severely hindering their progress in becoming fearless female leaders. In hearing their stories, we discovered that these and other women have a few common limiting beliefs:

- Life isn't fair.
- They have to go it alone.
- They should or must wait to be chosen.
- They can't break from tradition.

From each Shero featured in this book, you'll learn how they overcame these limiting beliefs and carved out their own paths, and how you can too.

It takes courage to share your gifts in a world that doesn't always seem to be inviting. Knowing this, our goal in writing this book is to help you find and adopt a new leadership model and a new way to share your gifts and ambitions with the world.

> ## Four Big Takeaways
>
> Before we dive into the details, we want you to take note of the four big takeaways from this book. These are the lessons we've learned and the wisdom we've garnered from the fearless female leaders we've interviewed, and this is how we believe you and other smart women like you can overcome the barriers to leadership. We recommend highlighting this section and coming back to it often:
>
> 1. Start focusing on what's most important (stop complaining about what's unfair).
> 2. Start developing success teams (stop trying to go it alone or prove your worth).
> 3. Start trusting that your gifts are wanted and needed (stop waiting to be chosen or recognized).
> 4. Start creating new ways to lead (stop trying to change today's archaic systems). Follow your own process, one step at a time. Never give up or give in.

* * * * *

Now that we have a foundation on which to build, let's get cracking on changing the current leadership paradigm. Let's not squander anyone's potential for a moment longer. Your fearless future awaits you. It's time to turn the page.

CHAPTER 2

Leadership Origin Stories: Recognizing Our Gifts

> When I dare to be powerful, to use my strength in the service of my vision,
> then it becomes less and less important whether I am afraid.
> ~Audre Lorde

Every fearless leader has a Leadership Origin Story—an early experience in their life when their leadership "superpowers" first came onto the scene. Given the undeveloped nature or immaturity of young and new leaders, or perhaps because of a lack of mentorship and guidance, these first experiences with being a leader are often difficult ones. Many are even unaware that the experiences are causing the formation of their views of leadership. Regardless, these early leadership experiences can have a profound impact on emerging leaders because they shape their beliefs, characters, and ambitions.

Writing and sharing your Leadership Origin Story helps you get in touch with the fearless leader within you. It also inspires other women and girls to see themselves as leaders. Most importantly, it assists you in reframing your experiences in ways that point to your superpowers. In turn, this supports you in integrating both the masculine and the feminine attributes of your leadership style so that you can become a more balanced fearless leader.

As the authors of this book, we aim to expose you to different ways of attaining this vital personal awareness of your leadership origins. How you choose to begin and what you pursue is of course your call. You are in charge. Our job is to guide, support, and challenge you and to make you more curious and open to discovery. For example, think back to your childhood and ponder these questions:

1. What did you want to be when you grew up and why?
2. When was the first time you realized you were a leader?
3. What was the outcome from that first leadership experience?
4. How did you process the lessons from that first leadership experience?

These are the very questions that we, your authors, used to unearth our Leadership Origin Stories. In the spirit of curiosity, openness, and transparency, we'd like to share with you the experiences that shaped who we are as fearless female leaders.

Leadership Origin Stories

Kathy McAfee
From Songleader to Creative Entrepreneur

I grew up as the second child and only girl in a family with four kids. My older brother, David, was born with cystic fibrosis, a very serious chronic disease with major respiratory complications and healthcare needs. Somehow, I got it in my head that it was "my job" to entertain, please, and distract others from the stress, worry, and concern that was ever present in our home. Because of my exuberance, which was seen as hyperactivity by adults, I failed my kindergarten entrance exam when I fell off the chair laughing. "She's not ready yet," they told my mother.

Since I couldn't go to school, my mother enrolled me in dance classes: tap, jazz, Hawaiian, and even a bit of ballet. There I played, learned, made friends, and had fun. Soon I was proclaiming that I wanted to be a professional dancer when I grew up. I continued to take dance classes until I was twelve years old. Then I found a new outlet, a new way of expressing my art and my leadership that helped me be accepted in school: songleading.

What is a songleader you ask? Well, we're like cheerleaders, only we do dance routines to music to build team spirit and support at athletic events. Ironically, I only recently recognized that the word "leader" is embedded in the name of this role. For many years, I downplayed (even hid) this part of my life because most people see cheerleading as a frivolous activity, not a "real" sport or a "real" leadership role. I hope that my story sets the record straight.

Serving as a songleader throughout middle school and high school was perhaps the first time my leadership skills came to the forefront. Working on a team with six to ten other talented and hardworking girls, we created beautiful outcomes. I excelled at choreography and music selection and quickly developed a knack for organizational leadership and discipline. Showmanship was one of my core strengths. Just like any sports team, we had our uniforms, practice schedules, and away games (thank you, carpool moms!). And we competed. In fact, our high school songleading team won the California State Championship. I still remember the opening moves from our fabulous routine to "Jump Shout Boogie."

But perhaps the achievement that I'm most proud of was when my cocaptain, Ann Schuster, and I wrote a "Spirit Constitution," a framework that called for representation and support for all sports, not just boys' football and basketball. We implemented this new vision by sending members of the larger spirit squad (cheer, song, drill, and mascots) to as many sporting events as we could—girls' volleyball, tennis, soccer, baseball, swimming, and wrestling events, you name it. We wanted to let all the athletes (boys, girls, and coed teams) from our school know that win or lose, we were proud of them, supported them, and appreciated them. Looking back on this now, this significantly changed how spirit squads in our school operated. This was an act of visionary leadership, and I wasn't even out of high school yet.

Then a remarkable event happened while I was attending cheerleading camp the summer before my senior year of high school. Out of more than five hundred students at the camp, Ann and I were selected to become instructors for the United Spirit Association. This was a big deal. Working with some of the most talented cheerleaders and songleaders in the country (including accomplished singer, dancer, and choreographer Paula Abdul), we taught summer camps to thousands of middle school and high school students. We even got paid, making us professional athletes.

Naturally, I assumed that this was the reason Stanford University accepted me out of thousands of applications to enroll as a freshman in their institution of higher learning. I was meant to become a "Dolly," the name they called their songleaders, and perform with the Stanford Band at their major athletic events. It became my mission to make the team. I wanted to take the Dollies to the next level of excellence and could see the opportunity to transform and professionalize that team. This became my calling. So I prepared for the audition. I was ready. I was confident. Deep down, I knew I had more relevant experience than any other applicant. My brother David, who played clarinet in the band, encouraged me to audition by telling me that I could make a positive difference.

I made the shortlist following the individual auditions. But what came next really shocked me. The next part of the audition was a group interview. Oddly, it was held at night at a rather seedy-looking event space. I remember seeing band members at all levels of the room, some even perching from the top of bookshelves. Music and alcohol flowed freely. At nineteen years of age, I didn't drink, so it was an awkward situation and something I'd never encountered before. I tried to remain cool, confident, and ladylike. I pretended like I fit in. Fortunately, David wasn't in the room, so he didn't have to see me struggle in this bizarre and demeaning situation.

The final winners would be notified in the morning, when they would be kidnapped from their dorm rooms by band members and whisked off to a celebratory breakfast. I wasn't awakened that morning. I wasn't chosen. But why?

I found out later that one band member, gleefully inebriated with alcohol, had shouted out, "She's a Nazi Youth!" The other student judges had quickly joined in on the false condemnation of my character and cast my application into the trash can. I was done. Apparently they didn't want someone like me who didn't drink and who took the audition so seriously. They preferred Dollies with more sex appeal—more bump and grind—and ones that fit their culture of rebellious fun. So not fair!

One of the students present in those wee hours of decision-making came to me a few days later to explain what had happened. He said that I shouldn't take it personally, that I was an excellent dancer, and that I'd make a great Dolly. He encouraged me to audition the following year. And so I did.

Knowing more about the rules of this game, including the unusual players and process, I prepared differently. I changed my costume, let my long hair down, put more jazz moves into my routine, and selected more contemporary music. I vowed to play and win by their rules and was confident that I'd make the team this time. And I was hopeful that by then the negative influences on the judging panel would've graduated and moved one. This turned out to be wishful thinking on my part.

I had underestimated the "culture" and long-standing "bad boy" reputation of the Stanford Band. They were hailed as the group that would get kicked off airplanes for unruly behavior. They weren't all bad, of course; after all, my beloved brother was part of this organization. Maybe it was my optimism or my naivete that made me think I could change this group's ethics, civility, and sense of fair play. But making that change wasn't within my influence or control. They remembered me alright. In their eyes, I was still a "Nazi Youth," even though I disguised myself with sex appeal. I got canned again. Now I was furious. This unfairness would not stand.

I appealed my case to dozens of university administrators, professors, athletic board members, and practically anyone who would listen to me. I told them about the injustice and abuse. I even claimed it was a form of student hazing, a clear violation of the student code of conduct that shouldn't be tolerated at Stanford. I was determined that those in power would see my side and take corrective action.

All the adults I spoke with—those who might've had power or influence—listened politely. But they did nothing. They just wanted me to go away. This wasn't a priority to them; it was "just" cheerleading, after all.

I spent the better part of my junior year in college trying to bring awareness and change to this unjust "tradition" on campus, including giving up opportunities to study abroad for my crusade. It was exhausting, but I was persistent, even dogged some might say. I didn't even let up after they compromised and gave me permission to start my own dance team to support men's basketball. I just couldn't let go of this injustice. I had to right this wrong.

Then, one beautiful day in mid-spring while I was sitting on a park bench outside the Cecil H. Green Library, another female student sat near me. She introduced herself as Chris and we began chatting. By the end of that conversation, I realized that I could let go of this fight and do something different. Chris and I saw an opportunity to launch a new student-run exercise program on campus. The existing one was practically a monopoly and was highly profitable, so there was room for some competition and choice. We came up with a great business name: "Stanford Aerobics: Mind and Body on the Move." It was a very successful and rewarding experience for me and our small team of student instructors.

Finding a new business partner and creating a new possibility for myself and others allowed me to finally let go of the loss. I redefined who I was as a leader and what I wanted to do with my leadership skills. This became the start of my life as an entrepreneur and a beautiful continuance of my life as a fearless female leader.

What I Learned from This Life Lesson

1. Even though it isn't fair, it's not what happens to you but what you do with it that makes the difference.
2. You don't have to go it alone, and you don't have to wait to be chosen. In fact, with a partner and a team you can be even more successful than by doing it all by yourself.
3. Breaking with tradition often produces a better result than continuing to buck the system.
4. Nothing can ultimately keep a true leader down, but a leader must know "when to hold 'em and when to fold 'em."

Rosemary Paetow
From Tennis Champion to Champion of Leaders

Most of my life, I've done what others said couldn't be done. I've had to think outside the box to get what I want and know which rules to break and which to follow to eliminate the barriers to my success. My mom and dad taught me what leadership is.

My family immigrated to the United States when I was four. When I started kindergarten, my mom said I was going to school for the both of us. You may be thinking that it was a lot to ask of a five-year-old, but the experience was fun, and it connected me to my mom. We were a team. Everything I learned at school I came home and taught her. The bonus was that this embedded in me the essential traits of learning, teaching, and leading.

My first taste of leadership happened at age eleven when my parents decided that I could take care of my active eight-year-old brother, cook the dinners, and clean the house so that my mom could work full time in support of the family. Society rarely looks upon babysitting or doing household chores as leadership training, but indeed it is. Looking back on this big-sister responsibility, I think of it as an unpaid internship. It wasn't such a bad gig (my brother was just the sweetest kid) until my parents decided to add a little extra to the mix that involved traveling to other towns to play tennis—with no parental supervision.

My dad was committed to the family unit and chose tennis as a sport the whole family could participate in. Every night after a ten-hour workday spent digging ditches, my dad took us out to the courts to practice. He told us that if we wanted to be good at something we must put the effort in; it's a sacrifice we must make in pursuit of excellence. As a kid this was lost on me because I just wanted to watch cartoons and play with my friends. But my dad had other plans for us. He wanted us to be the best, so we played and practiced every day unless it was raining.

While I loved my dad, I couldn't understand why he wasn't like other dads who let their kids do whatever they wanted. Why did we have to practice and practice? Of course, now I thank my dad for being such a dedicated parent who demanded the best from us and taught us to always strive to get to the next level. He was my coach, teacher, mentor, and most of all, my role model. In fact, most of my early leadership training came through my dad teaching me tennis.

Because there weren't enough competitions in our town, my dad found a youth tennis program in a neighboring city. Every other week there were tournaments for us to enter during the summer. The problem was that the city was more than an hour away from our home and I was too young to drive. So every other Wednesday, Thursday, and Friday, all summer long, my mom would drop my brother and me off at the tennis courts at 6:30 a.m. so that she could be at work by 8:00 a.m. Mom and Dad would then pick us up at 6 p.m., and we'd all make the long drive home. This was a grueling summer schedule for two kids (not to mention our parents), but this is what we did for the sake of tennis and family.

Aside from the long, boring days, another problem was that we didn't know anyone. The other kids and their parents were quite wealthy, as we were playing at private tennis clubs. Other than playing tennis, we didn't really have much in common with them. And there wasn't anything for us to do but wait for our matches, which took up only about two of the twelve hours we were stuck there.

It was so tedious sitting around and trying to entertain my now ten-year-old brother. I kept hoping my parents would think of some better plan. But after three months, we were still doing this crazy routine. So I devised a plan for my brother to make some friends who'd be willing to house him every other week, and I would do the same. That way I didn't have to keep entertaining him. When he was done playing tennis, he could go over to his friend's house where there was adult supervision. Best of all, we'd only have to get up early one day every other week, and we could have some fun to boot. It was a creative solution and it worked. Tennis encouraged my ability to think creatively.

As my dad recognized how responsible I was, he piled more leadership responsibilities onto my plate. In addition to working a full-time job as a foreman in a construction company, he also had a tennis shop where people could buy tennis paraphernalia. Because he wasn't available to run the shop until after 7 p.m., he asked me to oversee it. Yes, at the age of thirteen I became the store manager.

People I didn't know would come by and ask what kind of tennis racket they should buy. Their current skill level, the frequency of their play time, and their goals for their future skill level were all factors in determining the best racket for them. Because I couldn't see how they really played, and because people tend to exaggerate their abilities, I had to learn how to interpret what they said and assimilate it into their actual skill levels. Tennis taught me to determine how good someone is at their craft based on the way they talk about it and themselves, a skill I use today as a business coach and strategist.

When I was seventeen, the State of California changed the athletic code to allow females to play on a boys' team if that sport didn't have an equivalent girls' team. I tried out for the boys' team and beat them all, making me the first female in California to play on a boys' tennis team. This accomplishment should've been cause for celebration, but I soon realized the price I'd have to pay for being a fearless female trailblazer.

My coach decided to put me in the number two position on the team, so as not to demoralize the guys. I was asked to throw matches so the boys wouldn't feel humiliated being beaten by a woman. I remember the feeling of outrage when I was told to purposely lose. In my head I thought, *How dare you? Who are you to tell me that?* But what came out of my mouth was a timid and high pitched response: "Really?"

I struggled with this new reality but resolved to figure out how to play my own game and win. My father would've been outraged had he known. But did I tell him? Nope. I just handled it on my own.

Winning on the tennis court became my predictable outcome. But there were small losses that I endured for being so good at the game. For example, my teammates didn't watch my matches like they did with the guys. And dating wasn't easy. I remember a moment leading up to the senior prom. All my girlfriends had dates and were buying dresses and planning for the big night. I was waiting and waiting to be asked. It seemed that no boy wanted to go to the dance with a tall, athletic, competitive girl who beat every boy she ever faced on the tennis court. My mother encouraged me to stop waiting and ask a boy to the dance, so I asked a good friend of mine if he'd take me. He told me he couldn't because his out-of-town girlfriend would be jealous. You know, I didn't understand that answer at the time. I didn't realize what a threat I was to other girls. When I told my mom that John had said no, she said at least I took destiny into my hands and didn't wait around to be asked.

Even though I stayed home that night and watched TV, I still felt like a winner. Sometimes being better at something than others is lonely, but it sure beats the dreadful feeling of waiting for approval. My childhood years were spent focusing on improving myself, competing with myself to be better, and finding ways to have fun in the process.

Fast forward to when I was forty. My dad had just died, and I was at odds with my life. I was tired of working for companies that recognized and appreciated what I brought to the table but weren't willing to promote me to the executive table (or even pay me fairly). My head hurt from hitting the glass ceiling again and again. I wanted something different. My parents had always told me that I had the talent to do anything I set my mind to and that I'd be successful. It was time for me to break with tradition and carve out my own path. But how?

To figure it out, I went back to my roots in tennis. I felt this was where I might find a thread, an idea to pull on for my next gig. So I headed to Scottsdale, Arizona, to a very prestigious resort and tennis facility. The pro at this resort had taught Venus and Serena Williams. He knew talent when he saw it, so I knew I could trust him to tell me how to improve my game. He rallied with me on the court, shot some videos of me playing, and then we went to his lounge area for the evaluation. I was a bit nervous because of his credentials.

"Before we look at your game," he said, "I need to know who taught you to play tennis."

Surprised by this request, I asked him why. He said that he had never seen such a picture-perfect form as mine and that whoever taught me should be thanked. It took everything in me not to cry as I answered, "My dad."

Sitting on that leather couch in the sweltering heat of an Arizona summer, I finally understood the gift my dad had given me. He just wouldn't settle for "good enough." He demanded my best and he pulled it out of me. He was an awesome coach and teacher who demanded that I put in the effort if I wanted to be good, and because of him I developed the discipline, focus, and drive to do so. My dad saw my greatness, and he opened the doors for me to become a better tennis player.

From that moment on, I decided that I would no longer wait to be picked, no longer wait to be promoted to the executive suite. I would take what tennis and my dad taught me and use it to start and run my own business. I would be the CEO of my own firm. My practice is and always has been based on what I was trained into. Combining my skill in translating what I'm taught through lectures, books, and coaching with my skill in recognizing the gap between where a person is and where they can go allows for more rapid and seamless growth.

As I reflect on my Leadership Origin Story, I can honestly say that it's been a joyous and scary ride. I want to share with other women what I learned along the way and how I embodied all that my dad and mom taught me about how to lead. I hold dear these valuable leadership lessons that tennis taught me through my mentor—my beloved dad and my guide—and my loving mom.

What I Learned from This Life Lesson

1. Excellence matters. Be bold and do your best with anything you touch.
2. Confidence counts. Believe in yourself and recognize that what you bring to the table is needed and wanted in this world.
3. Never give up or give in. Think outside the box, and the answers will come to you. Solve what's yours to solve in unique and unusual ways and have the wisdom to ask for help when it isn't yours to solve.
4. Forge your own path. The journey is yours, so know which rules to break. Life may not be fair, but you can play your own game and win!

* * * * *

Discovering the true source of our Leadership Origin Stories is hard to do all by ourselves. We often get stuck in old narratives and limiting beliefs. We need more tools and guidance to help us see ourselves differently. And that's what you'll find in the next chapter. We'll assist you in navigating the introspective journey necessary to discover more of who you are, what you care about, and who you can become. Ultimately, it's about recognizing that *you* are the leader of your life and your career and, if you so choose, a leader of people and organizations. If you're feeling trepidatious, that's okay. We'll be right by your side every step of the way.

CHAPTER 3

Owning Your Leadership Potential

We are the authors of our lives. We write our own daring endings.
~Brene Brown, excerpt from the poem
"Manifesto of the Brave and Brokenhearted"

In her book *The Secret of the Shadow*, Debbie Ford talks about the power of owning our whole self. The sum of our lives, from the families we were born into to what we've accomplished (or could've accomplished), is a part of each of our stories; each aspect is a building block that makes up the unique being each of us is. Basing her ideas on Carl Jung's research that disowning parts of our being creates a shadow under which we form the limiting beliefs that reinforce that shadow, Ford postulates that to own ourselves we must first own the parts of ourselves that we dislike. And when we own all aspects of our being—the good and the bad—we free ourselves to create anything and live and lead a life of our own design. We can be happy right here, right now.

In this chapter, we offer several powerful tools that help you not only identify the things that are slowing you down, tripping you up, and sometimes even stopping you completely, but also "rewrite" them in empowering ways. We start by providing a tool you can use to uncover what formed you into the leader you are today (your Leadership Origin Story). Then, to help keep you in check, we offer suggestions for how you can discover the inner barriers (we call them leadership shadows) and limiting beliefs you've created.

Once you recognize your faulty limitations and your shadows, you no longer need to be bound by them. Facing them opens the opportunity to create a fresh start. You do that with a tool we created called The Fearless Leader Manifesto, which embodies your values, what you're committed to, and what people can count on you for. In other words, it's a short description that captures your essence and reflects who you are as a leader and how you intend to lead, thus becoming the new declaration of who you are as a leader.

Your Leadership Origins

Elizabeth Gilbert, author of *Eat Pray Love*, points out that one of the oddest tricks that the universe plays on human beings is to bury strange jewels within us all. The frustration comes when we don't see them or know how to mine them. Before that's possible, it's important to know where we come from and what we think is in our way. Only then can we reframe our stories as jewels or gifts.

There are several ways to approach this process. You can make a list of the most important events in your life that shaped you (think of the stories you consistently tell about your childhood), write short paragraphs about the key events that shaped your life and perspectives (we call them Glimpses), or describe your aspirations and make a list of what's gotten in the way of reaching them. To make your process as easy as possible, we've developed several specific methods, all of which are designed to eliminate the limiting beliefs that might be telling you, "I can't do this; I'm not a writer." It's completely up to you to decide which method works for you, either alone or in combination. Remember, this isn't about writing a Pulitzer Prize novel. This is about getting the essence of you down on paper.

The first method is to write a summary of your life, a way to remind you of what makes you you. It can be in outline or timeline form. Naturalist and acclaimed poet David Whyte, best known for his book *The Heart Aroused: Poetry and the Preservation of the Soul in Corporate America*, has a beautiful way of doing this. He uses "I am from" poems, a common teaching practice stemming from George Ella Lyons's poem "Where I'm From," to complete the phrase "I am from" using prompts such as these:

- Who your parents are
- Where you were born
- Where you grew up
- What impacted you growing up
- Where you went to school
- What jobs you've held
- Your immediate family today

When coauthor Rosemary first did this exercise, she began this way:

- "I am from Maria and Herbert, immigrants to the United States."
- "I am from my mother, who sent me to school saying, 'You're learning for the both of us. Come home and teach me what you learned.'"

What Rosemary learned in writing down just those first sentences is that she had been taking on the "learning to teach" role from the time she was five. Now, anytime she goes into a lecture or a program, she integrates the material beforehand so that when she walks out the door, she's ready to teach. That's a powerful gift. She also learned that she thought of herself as "different" or "separate" from others. English was a second language to her, and that made her feel like she didn't belong and that she was on her own (forming one of her leadership shadows).

Once you make your own outline, you can look for the limiting beliefs that are hiding just below the surface, the way Rosemary noticed the impact of English as a second language. Or you can go directly to identifying your limiting beliefs, those negative things you say about yourself in your head (*I'm not strong enough; I'm not pretty enough*).

Another creative method to understand your Leadership Origin Story and what you're made of is writing what coauthor Kathy calls "Glimpses." She reconnected with her past by identifying specific life and career experiences that impacted her and writing them down—without judgment—into very short passages. To her, these excerpts from her life became like scenes from a movie. Stepping back from the experiences and sharing them with coauthor Rosemary allowed Kathy to see themes, threads, and throughlines. It surprised her that the actual writing of her Leadership Origin Story seemed to flow from her without struggle. And when she was moved to tears as she read the section about sitting on the park bench outside of the library, she knew she had found what needed to be shared with the world.

Again, there are many ways to approach this. Don't limit yourself. This process will help you uncover your gifts and what's holding you back.

Your Conscious and Unconscious Limiting Beliefs

As we've already learned, there are many barriers to women's leadership advancement. Most of the ones we discovered in our survey and have discussed thus far are external. But equally important are the internal barriers: our beliefs (conscious and unconscious) and the way we talk to ourselves (our inner critics).

A "shadow belief," a term first coined by Jung, is an *unconscious* belief, one that is hidden from our view but influences and drives negative behaviors and undesired results in our lives. Shadow beliefs rob us of our power by fueling our inner critics. A limiting belief, on the other hand, is a *conscious* belief, one that is a temporary state of mind that stops us from achieving what we want; it is a filter through which we interpret our experiences.

We can also think of a limiting belief as a decision we make (consciously or unconsciously) about ourselves or the world. The intention of limiting beliefs is to protect us, but sometimes they outlive their usefulness and prevent us from reaching our full potential. The good news is that we can clear out those limiting beliefs and make new decisions, ones that support us and help us move forward in more positive and productive ways. We call these "empowering new beliefs."

To gain this type of new belief system, it's a healthy practice to periodically examine and challenge our limiting beliefs, both conscious and unconscious. Meet Toni, for example, who was being held back by hers.

A Glimpse

Despite balancing a good career and a happy family, Toni was holding on to the limiting belief that she could never be as successful as her colleagues because she didn't finish college. She believed that the lack of a diploma would prevent her from rising in the leadership ranks of her company and industry. However, at this point in her career, it didn't make economic sense to go back to college to finish her degree. She was content to continue to do the work she loved for clients she adored—until the department head announced that he'd be retiring. Sadly, the successor he'd been grooming died unexpectedly. That left the succession seat vacant. Toni wished that she might be considered, but she didn't even apply because she didn't have a degree.

Uncovering Your Leadership Shadow

If you've studied psychology at all, you've no doubt come across the concept of "the shadow." For the purposes of our discussion on women's leadership, we want to focus especially on leadership shadows.

What is a "leadership shadow" you ask? According to Dr. William Sparks, Professor of Leadership at the McColl School of Business at Queens University in Charlotte, North Carolina, and the author of *Actualized Leadership: Meeting Your Shadow, Maximizing Your Potential*, the term describes the three fear-based reactions that leaders exhibit under stress. Based on the seminal work of Jung and his concept of the shadow, leadership shadows correspond to each of three motive needs that drive our leadership styles:

1. The Achiever Style: fear of failure
2. The Affirmer Style: fear of rejection
3. The Asserter Style: fear of betrayal[20]

Dr. Sparks defines the term *leadership shadow* as "the extreme, negative manifestation of our positive drivers."[21] These shadows are based on irrational thoughts and unfounded fears that seem like the truth, and they stay alive by masking our core beliefs. Because no one is immune from stress, we are all vulnerable to workplace triggers that can activate our leadership shadows, resulting in career-limiting moves such as micromanaging, avoiding conflict, or refusing to trust others. To get a snapshot of your leadership profile, your leadership shadows, and the kinds of qualities and behaviors you're likely to exhibit when you're at your best and at your worst, you can take a free assessment at www.ALPfree.com.

When working to identify our leadership shadows, the goal isn't to eliminate them but integrate and manage them. Our shadows are an indelible part of us. Getting in touch with them starts with asking these three eternal questions, as identified by Dr. Sparks in his certification trainings:

1. Am I wanted?
2. Am I worthy?
3. Am I safe?

---

[20] William L. Sparks, *Actualized Leadership: Meeting Your Shadow & Maximizing Your Potential* (Alexandria, VA: Society for Human Resource Management Press, 2019), 12, 30–31.
[21] Sparks, 30.

All of us have had early childhood experiences with some degree of trauma. How we processed those experiences had an impact on our developing personalities and core needs. They also set in motion the development of our leadership shadows. Many of us are still wrestling with one or more of the three eternal questions.

Shadow work is deep work, so you may wish to ponder these questions related to the current state of your leadership shadow as a more comfortable starting point:

- What is your relationship to failure? Is it okay for you to make mistakes? Do you have to be perfect and have a flawless scorecard to be successful in your eyes and those of the people you work with?
- What is your relationship with rejection? What comes up when you and your ideas are declined or ignored by others? Does it feel personal and hurtful? Do you become angry or cynical? Does it make you not want to try again?
- What is your relationship with betrayal? Can you really trust anyone? How can you be certain they won't abandon you or throw you under the proverbial bus?

Examining our leadership shadows helps us make better leadership decisions. It supports us in becoming more self-actualized leaders who are capable of creating dynamic team cultures. Evolving in this way is useful not only for ascending to higher levels of leadership responsibility but also for thriving once that's achieved.

Making Peace with Your Leadership Shadow

Shadows are a part of each of us. Left unattended they can hijack our thoughts, feelings, and behaviors. To control that process, we first need to bring our leadership shadows into our conscious thoughts, then make new choices that empower our dreams rather than sabotage them.

Toni's leadership profile is the Affirmer Style. Her leadership shadow is fear of rejection. So it was only natural for her to avoid any chance of being rejected due to her college diploma issue. As a result, she found herself not speaking up in meetings. She felt small despite her 5'10" stature and athletic frame.

When we asked Toni how she felt when she thought about her leadership shadow, she said, "I become very quiet and step into the background to hide. It makes me feel inferior to others who have a college degree."

Then we asked Toni how she'd feel if it were impossible to think that thought. She replied, "I would be exactly who I am: a very intellectual and emotionally intelligent person." She went on to share that she realizes a college education isn't a replacement for experience and time. She learns every single day, and she's always working on herself. "College is a starting point, not a destination nor a gauge for intelligence," she realized.

With this new energy and inspiration, Toni was able to manage her shadow and turn her limiting belief into an empowering thought. She articulated it as, "I am a very capable, smart person. Life is an education. I don't need a degree to help people and provide them with my gifts." With this new decision and way of looking at herself and the world, Toni was ready to take the next step in her leadership journey by applying an essential tool from The Fearless Leader program.

And that's exactly what Toni did. She busted through her limiting beliefs and replaced them with empowering new ones. Then she used The Fearless Leader Manifesto to capture how she wanted to be known as a leader. Once Toni completed it and shared it with her team, things started to change. She was selected as one of the new leaders of the practice.

During the transition, the outgoing leader said to Toni with delight, "Where have you been all this time?"

"Mike, I've been here for ten years," she told him. But inside, she thought to herself, *Yes, I've been here many years and I've done a great job, but I've been afraid of being in the spotlight. No more hiding. It's my time to lead.*

That's what can happen when you unleash the fearless leader within you.

Creating Your Fearless Leader Manifesto

The Fearless Leader Manifesto is a one-page declaration and visual representation of how we intend to show up as leaders, and as human beings. It encapsulates our values, beliefs, passions, and ideals, all in one compelling design. It communicates the depth of who we are. By developing your Fearless Leader Manifesto, you empower yourself and give clarity and confidence to those you lead. It also helps you:

- know your intrinsic worth,
- clarify your values,
- communicate your leadership philosophy,
- lead more authentically, and
- connect with your purpose and experience more joy.

> **Five Steps to Creating Your Fearless Leader Manifesto**
>
> 1. Get in touch with your core values
> 2. Discover your personal brand
> 3. Get creative
> 4. Declare and share
> 5. Fuel your joy

Step #1: Get in Touch with Your Core Values

Our values are the things we believe are important in the way we live and work. They determine our priorities and, deep down, are probably the measures we use to determine whether our lives are turning out the way we want them to. If another person goes against our values, it upsets us. When creating your Fearless Leader Manifesto, then, it's important to select your true values, not just the ones you say you value or what your employer or your parents think you should value. What do you truly value?

Let's be honest. It can be very challenging to live according to our values, especially as a member of a group or a collective. We see incongruences every day at work. Company values are revered and beautifully displayed on posters that hang in the hallways, but they are regularly dismissed and ignored. Decisions made about profits, policies, and practices are often out of alignment with corporate values, which can be discouraging. But don't let that stop you from examining, owning, and living your personal values.

Leadership coach and thought leader David O'Brien offers a simple but powerful exercise called the Values Clarity Worksheet,[22] which you can download from his WorkChoice Solutions website. It asks you to select the top five values that are most important to you in your work as a leader and influencer. You get to choose from a long list of concepts including harmony, accuracy, responsibility, safety, trust, loyalty, status, inclusion, and winning. Narrowing the list to only five can be difficult, and it requires that you thoughtfully choose.

O'Brien recommends going through the list a second time, this time picking what your team or colleagues believe is most important to you. Looking at these two lists side by side can reveal some interesting differences. Keep in mind that your words and deeds reflect how others perceive your values and that others often project their values onto you.

Another good resource to help you get in touch with your core values is The Fearless Leader Manifesto Journal Exercise. It's designed as a quick response, thought-starter tool to help you identify values that your thinking mind might otherwise not allow you to say out loud. It's as easy as filling in the blanks. Give it a go.

- I am:
- I will:
- I do not tolerate:
- I believe:

---

[22] David O'Brien, "The Values Clarity Worksheet," WorkChoice Solutions, accessed August 9, 2023, http://www.workchoicesolutions.com/images/The_Values_Clarity_Worksheet.pdf.

- I cherish:
- I lead by:
- I role model:
- I accept:
- You can count on me to:
- I will always:
- This is who I am as a:
- I'll know it's time to go when:
- My work matters because:
- I will not:
- I stand for:
- [write your own custom prompts]

You can access The Fearless Leader Manifesto Journal Exercise by scanning the QR code at the end of this chapter.

Step #2: Discover Your Personal Brand

The concept of personal branding is a fairly new phenomenon. It was first coined in 1997 by author and thought leader Tom Peters. In his many speeches and writings, Peters is fond of reminding us that no matter what industry we work in or where we live, we're all CEOs of our own personal brands, and that means we must market ourselves just as vigorously as we would any product or service. Yet so many professionals don't. They leave their personal brands to chance and don't manage them consistently. Imagine what would happen if the Apple brand were ignored or mismanaged? We'd be shocked and disappointed, and its sales and stock price could tumble.

Whether you know it or not, you currently have a personal brand. Your default brand is your reputation—how others see you and think of you. It's what they've come to expect from you based on past interactions, including your behaviors, image, affiliations, social media activity, accomplishments, mistakes, and inconsistencies. Taking an external audit of your personal brand requires listening to some difficult feedback. It isn't easy to have people hold up a mirror and give you critical feedback, but you need to know how you're presently perceived if you desire to improve.

The good news about personal branding is that *you* get to decide how you want to be known professionally. It's your brand, after all, so you are the author of it. And you are responsible for living up to that brand through your daily actions and interactions.

There are a few other important things to know about personal branding. Your job title is not your brand. Don't stake your claim on being known as "2nd VP." Your company isn't your brand either, although there should be some alignment and affinity. If you're currently in transition, out of work, or retired, that doesn't mean you no longer have a brand; you're much more than your current circumstance. If you're a mom, caregiver, or wife, that's wonderful, but that isn't your personal brand either; these are important roles you play, but they aren't representative of who you are. Your personal brand will evolve and grow with you, so don't box yourself in.

Arthur Samuel Joseph, author and creator of the Vocal Awareness Institute, has a lot to say about personal branding. He challenges us not to merely *present* ourselves, but to *be* ourselves. In his book *Vocal Leadership*, he offers an exercise called the Persona Statement, a wonderful tool to help us discover the essence of our personal brands. "The Persona Statement is a way to remove our mask and reveal the Deeper Self in a more sovereign way," Joseph writes. It's "the canvas on which we masterfully create the image of our authentic Self. As we learn to embody our Persona Statement, we are better able to confront our two greatest fears: abandonment and claiming our greatness."[23]

Personal branding work requires us to go beyond the surface. We can't attempt to create a persona in someone else's image. We must make an intentional choice to be who we truly are, to stop comparing ourselves to others, and to honor our differences and our unique gifts. So develop, invest, and embody your true essence. It's the core of your personal brand, and it's already inside you.

---

[23] Arthur Samuel Joseph, *Vocal Leadership: 7 Minutes a Day to Communication Mastery* (New York: McGraw Hill, 2014), 43–47.

If you're interested in replacing your standard thirty-second elevator pitch with a positioning statement that's both authentic and strategic, we recommend reading *Defining YOU: How Smart Professionals Craft the Answers To: Who Are You? What Do You Do? How Can You Help Me?* by Mark LeBlanc, Kathy McAfee, and Henry DeVries. Inside this book is a tool called the Defining Paragraph,[24] which is a strategic framework that helps you determine and communicate your areas of expertise and the types of leadership work you seek now and in the future. It's an empowering process to experience, and it results in a highly useful and flexible tool for positioning you as a leader in your field. Remember, people can't read your mind, and they don't always know what you want to do next. It's up to you to communicate clearly and concisely. And while you're at it, why not use the language of leadership when you speak about yourself, your work, and your ambitions.

Step #3: Get Creative

This is where creating your Fearless Leader Manifesto starts getting fun. Your thoughts, feelings, empowering beliefs, values, Persona Statement, essence, and even your leadership shadows become your artist's palette, and the colors are what bring your Manifesto to life. Even if you don't consider yourself a creative person, you can take this step. (Note: This might be a limiting belief you need to bust through.)

The basic idea of Step 3 is to convert the words and ideas from Step 1 into a graphic presentation. We're not talking about boring PowerPoint slides here, so don't dumb it down. Make it spectacular, like you are. Many of our clients use Canva to develop their Fearless Leader Manifestos. Some hire professional graphic designers to help them create something visual. Some take the vision board approach, tearing pictures and headlines from magazines and pasting them on a

---

[24] Mark LeBlanc, Kathy McAfee, and Henry DeVries, *Defining YOU: How Smart Professionals Craft the Answers To: Who Are You? What Do You Do? How Can You Help Me?* (Oceanside, CA: Indie Books International, 2018).

poster board. Others use original photos and connect the images with their stories.

When coauthor Kathy took this step of creating her Manifesto, she took a photograph of a mature Japanese maple tree planted in her front garden. She made a connection between the tree and how she wanted to be known professionally: as a leader who can create environments and microclimates in which others can blossom and thrive, resulting in outcomes of splendor. Every time she walks by that tree, she smiles and reflects on the beauty and potential of her own essence and leadership ambition.

How you bring your Fearless Leader Manifesto to life visually is completely up to you. Get creative, take a risk, and create something original. Your Manifesto can be as unique and one-of-a-kind as you are!

You can see examples of Manifestos that others have created while participating in The Fearless Leader program, including Toni's, by scanning the QR code at the end of this chapter. Use these as inspirations and energizers, but don't copy them. Your Fearless Leader Manifesto deserves to reflect who you are and how you intend to show up as a leader—your authentic self.

Step #4: Declare and Share

It's now time to share your Fearless Leader Manifesto with the world. It deserves more than just a posting on some social media site. It needs to be part of your professional portfolio and should be considered as valuable as your resume, biography, letters of reference, client testimonials, awards, certificates, degrees, and website. In many cases, this step is the most powerful because it's a creative and visual way to reflect your values, aspirations, personality, and leadership vision. There are many possible uses for your Fearless Leader Manifesto:

- If you're applying for a new job, consider presenting your Manifesto during your interview with the hiring manager. They'll have a greater sense of who you are and what kind of leader you'll be.

- ✷ If you're having a networking coffee chat with someone, consider sharing your Manifesto as a way of sharing more of who you are. Ask them about their Manifesto.
- ✷ If you're being introduced to a team as a new leader, include your Manifesto in your onboarding meetings and town hall meetings, if you have them. It may not be protocol, but it would be a lot more refreshing than the boring slide-showing, talking-head kind of leader. That's not you anyway. You are something different.
- ✷ If you have a website, consider including your Manifesto on the About Us page. Include your photo, a personal written statement, and your fantastically creative Manifesto image. Give the image a strong SEO coding so it will come up in searches for the phrase "leadership manifesto."

You can also use your Fearless Leader Manifesto design as background art for your social media sites, which beats the heck out of using stock photography. And let's not forget the opportunity to print and frame your Manifesto and hang it in your office and at home. Your peers and family need and want to know more about you—the real you.

Other applications include using parts of your Manifesto in written and spoken formats, such as in your elevator pitch, biography, website, and Leadership Origin Story. And remember to use aspects of your Manifesto to make your LinkedIn About section more real and compelling. We recommend writing in the first person rather than speaking about yourself in the third person as if you weren't in the room. Remember, you are more than your resume. Infinitely more.

Step #5: Fuel Your Joy

The final step in creating a powerful Fearless Leader Manifesto is to fuel your joy. This must happen daily. It's both easy and important to do, and it can take as little as eight minutes. The secret is to do something you truly love—something that makes you smile, laugh, and feel good. Fueling your joy involves stepping away from the computer, putting down the technology, getting out into nature, looking up and around, breathing in the fresh air, and taking time for yourself. Recharge. Eight minutes, dear reader. That's all it takes to fuel your joy.

Anna Hall, founder and CEO of The Purpose Equation, believes wholeheartedly that joy makes an impact on our ability to connect with our innate purpose. In turn, that connection drives us to give and receive meaning daily. Joy, if you will, bolsters the resilience of the human spirit.

Joy is essential not only to fueling our purpose but to making us better versions of ourselves. Without joy, we cannot be the leaders we aspire to be. All work and no play make Jack a dull boy (and Jill, too). Without joy we are at risk of burnout, distress, boredom, and loss of confidence. Without joy our connection to our purpose weakens. Your Fearless Leader Manifesto—and your future—depends on your ability to fuel your joy daily.

The bottom line is this: If you don't like the story you're in, leave it. Create something that makes you happy and brings you joy.

* * * * *

Congratulations! You've made it through part 1. You've learned about the power of creating your Leadership Origin Story, rooted up some of the barriers to your expression of leadership and how to reframe them, and were introduced to The Fearless Leader Manifesto to create a stunning pictorial representation of who you are as a leader.

We invite you now to move into part 2 where we provide additional tools to help you show up as the leader you want to be. We'll introduce you to eight great attributes of fearless leadership. You'll also be introduced to a new model of leadership that is more balanced and holistic. We call it The Shero's Journey. Prepare to be inspired.

Fear less and LEAD MORE

Download the journal exercise to begin your Fearless Leader Manifesto.
See examples from other fearless leaders.

Access bonus gifts here:
fearlessleaderbooks.com/bonuses

PART 2

INSPIRED SOLUTIONS:
Owning Your Story & Becoming More Fearless

CHAPTER 4

Embodying Attributes of Fearless Leadership

If they don't give you a seat at the table, bring a folding chair.
~Shirley Chisholm

Despite the barriers and disadvantages that women continue to face in the workplace, we must recognize that women have changed the conversation about leadership. Women have positively influenced the course of business and government and will continue to do so. Why? Because women bring a unique set of qualities to the leadership conversation. And while every woman is uniquely different, our biology and DNA cannot be refuted. We have inherent strengths that are different from men. We really do have superpowers—emotional, intellectual, social, and even physical ones. After all, who else could endure nine months of drastic bodily changes only to have to endure hours of physical anguish at the finish line to continue the human race?

As author Diane Mariechild puts it, "A woman is the Full Circle. A woman's power is to create . . . to nurture . . . to heal . . . to transform."[25]

---

[25] Diane Mariechild, *The Inner Dance: A Guide to Spiritual and Psychological Unfolding* (Freedom, CA: Crossing Press, 1987), 168.

So why aren't we creating, nurturing, healing, and transforming at the highest levels in the business world? Why are women still the underdogs of the workforce?

Maybe it's because the current model of leadership is broken and imbalanced. Like a crumbling bridge, the infrastructure of our current leadership model is in desperate need of repair or replacement. Despite all the inroads that women have made in the last fifty years, the current model continues to favor men. Male biology, male attributes, and male role models continue to dominate in modern society. And if we are totally honest, the current model favors White men.

Don't worry, men, we aren't trying to replace you. We just want to stand with you as equals, as collaborators, as partners in business and at home. We know that men who are willing make terrific caregivers, fathers, sons, husbands, and full partners in business and in life. Yet why won't more men make room for more women at the leadership table?

What's the solution? Repair? Replace? Reinvent? As authors of this book, we admit that we don't have all the answers, but we do have some questions and ideas for you to consider. Together we can cocreate a new model for leadership: one that empowers people of all pronouns and seeks to create diversity of leadership and equity of opportunity for all people regardless of gender, race, color, age, or identity; one that models inclusive and encouraging leadership that's fairer and more effective in the long run for the benefit of the whole of society. It's time to think big.

To keep this simple, let's start by creating a shared list of attributes for fearless leadership. What does it take to be a fearless leader? What are the attributes they must bring to the table to lead effectively and have others confidently follow them?

Throughout history, our leaders and our celebrated heroes have possessed specific attributes that led them to succeed. These attributes are well-documented and include traits such as boldness, confidence, wisdom, and humor. We believe that women are adding to the attributes needed to succeed in today's world with gifts such as intuition, compassion, resonance, and resilience. We propose that these eight great attributes of fearless leadership, which integrate both masculine and feminine leadership styles, be adopted by companies, taught in schools, and encouraged in children—our future leaders.

Eight Great Attributes of Fearless Leadership

1. Boldness
2. Intuition
3. Compassion
4. Confidence
5. Resonance
6. Resilience
7. Wisdom
8. Humor

Let's unpack each of these eight great attributes. For each one, we'll discuss why it's important for leaders, how men and women express it differently, and how you can cultivate it in yourself, your team, and your family to become a whole leader who is fearless.

Attribute #1: Boldness
(Fearless, Courageous, Gutsy, Audacious)

Boldness is a trait that men know and embody. From an early age, they're taught not to show their pain, their hurt, or their fear because it can be used against them. It can be weaponized. So for men, boldness looks like a "game face." It looks like persevering in the face of big obstacles. And they make it look easy. As Tom Hanks's character says in *A League of Their Own*, "There's no crying in baseball."[26]

Men know boldness takes courage. Yet when Black women express boldness in the workplace, even if just to share their ideas, they're often confronted with microaggressions and labeled as an "angry Black woman." In her article "What Society Gets Wrong About the 'Angry Black Woman' Stereotype," Amira Barger explains, "For Black women like me, or women of other historically excluded groups, we have the unfortunate experience of what experts call 'double jeopardy.' We experience discrimination and inequity for two marginalized identities—being women and being racialized. This workplace-induced stress causes physiological changes to our bodies and can result in

---

[26] *A League of Their Own*, directed by Penny Marshall (1992; Culver City, CA: Columbia Pictures, 2004), DVD.

chronic changes and a shorter lifespan. For us as Black women, the repercussions of daring to emote—to 'be angry'—are as consequential as those for remaining silent about our plight. Our health and literal lives are at stake."[27]

So what's a more balanced, healthier view of boldness? We define it as having the courage to be vulnerable, to trust that the people on our teams will do the right thing even when no one's looking, to persevere in the face of disagreement (or as we like to say, being unstoppable), and to know when to collaborate and when to take charge. In other words, to boldly go where no one has gone before. (Three cheers to *Star Trek*!)

What can we women do to develop this keener sense of boldness? It's simple: Stop seeking agreement. Stop needing to be liked. Be okay with rejection; it won't kill us. Speak up, speak out, and ask for what we want and need, and support others who need our advocacy. As you read in chapter 2, coauthor Kathy cultivated this attribute at a very young age. It took many years for her to realize that boldness was part of her leadership persona.

Attribute #2: Intuition
(Trusting Your Gut, Spiritual Courage, Discernment)

Intuition is a trait that women are intimately familiar with. Whenever there's not enough information to make an informed decision, women, especially when their children's safety is an issue, will trust their instincts. To avoid the stigma of being "illogical," many very successful male CEOs credit the positive results they get from following their intuition as "luck" or "trusting their gut."

Most women have a well-developed sense of intuition. Some, like coauthor Rosemary, "back up" their intuition with logic. Others, like

---

[27] Amira Barger, "What Society Gets Wrong About the 'Angry Black Woman' Stereotype," MSNBC, April 17, 2023, https://www.msnbc.com/know-your-value/business-culture/what-society-gets-wrong-about-angry-black-woman-stereotype-n1304353.

coauthor Kathy, have been trained to ignore their intuition because others label it as "woo-woo" or frivolous:

A Glimpse

Kathy was facing a dilemma that required her to make an important career and life decision. A former mentor and boss was recruiting her to relocate back to her home state of California to take a new job in a new industry. The problem was, she had just been offered an exciting promotion at her current company, Maybelline, which was based in Memphis, Tennessee. It made sense to stay in Memphis where she had developed relationships and a positive career track. And yet her heart was pulling her to California.

She flew home for a visit over Christmas holiday to visit her brother David, whose health was failing, and to determine the best course of action for her career: make the logical decision and stay in Memphis with an assured career path, or follow her heart and move back to California where there would be many unknowns (new people, new accountabilities, and the uncertainty around her brother's health). The night before she had to commit, Kathy went to sleep with a heavy heart, asking for the spiritual courage to make the right choice.

The next morning she awoke with crystal clarity and a sense of peace. Her intuition told her to accept the new job and move back to California. It turned out to be the best decision for her. She was able to spend the last six months of her brother's life with him. A year later she met the love of her life and future husband, Byron. And the icing on the cake? Her new company offered her an exciting three-year job assignment in Europe.

None of this would've been possible if Kathy had followed her typical path and chosen logic over intuition. This time, Kathy had the spiritual courage to follow her heart. This time, following her intuition, she made a decision that radically changed her life. Luck? Hardly.

Cultivating intuition requires trust, feeling, listening, and discernment. Being able to hear and then trust your intuitive inner voice is essential. To do that, first silence all the inner noise (the judgment, the inner critic, the "but that's not logical" voice) through mindfulness, meditation, deep breaths, and/or exercise. Then pick something that has no right answer, take a guess (from your gut), and see how often you made a good call. Rinse and repeat.

You can start with simple things like, "Should I turn right or left?" Don't try to explain it or look for validation, just follow your intuition. Don't worry about offending someone else. If something feels wrong, don't go there. This might just save your life.

The more we can trust ourselves, the better choices we will make. The better choices we make, the better leaders we become.

Attribute #3: Compassion
(Empathy, Humanity, Emotional Intelligence, Kindness)

Compassion is a trait that women naturally have. When men get older, they gain compassion too. It has to do with brain chemistry. Neuroscience tells us that the right side of the brain is where compassion resides and where women operate from. As a man gets older, the bridge between the left and right hemispheres of his brain expands, giving him more access to the feeling, compassionate side of the brain.[28] For a woman, one of the benefits of going through menopause is that this brain bridge expands, giving her more access to the left side of the brain, the part that holds logic and objectivity.[29]

Please understand that compassion is connected to estrogen, and logic is connected to testosterone. All men and all women have both hormones. It's just that men in their youth generally have more testosterone and therefore more access to the logical side of the brain, while women in their youth have more estrogen and therefore more access

---

[28] Louann Brizendine, The Male Brain: A Breakthrough Understanding of How Men and Boys Think (New York: Harmony Books, 2011).
[29] Louann Brizendine, *The Female Brain* (New York: Harmony Books, 2007).

to the compassion side of the brain. But that doesn't mean that young women can't learn logic, nor does it mean that young men can't learn compassion. It just means that these traits come easier with the hormone levels affiliated with them.

Why is compassion important in the workplace? Because we're no longer in the Industrial Age when cruelty and indifference were the hallmarks of leaders. Because no matter how much automation and artificial intelligence take over, business is still about people. And people have feelings. Compassion is designed to bring out the very best in us—the better versions of ourselves, the goodness.

There are two reasons people strive to be more compassionate leaders: to be better human beings and to bring out the best in their teams. The more people feel that their leaders, managers, and colleagues care about them, the more they'll remain loyal in times of hardships and work harder. As they say, "You catch more flies with honey than with vinegar."

A Glimpse

Coauthor Rosemary had a conversation with her colleague Sally, who shared that she was worried about her mother. After a bit of gentle probing by Rosemary, Sally shared the news that her mom had liver cancer. Despite a very large project they were working on together, Rosemary convinced Sally to go see her mother and assured her that she'd provide coverage while she was gone. "You need to go. You need to be there with your mom," Rosemary encouraged her. But when Rosemary went to tell the boss-man, he argued that it was bad timing for this employee to leave and that it would jeopardize the project. He pushed Rosemary to reverse her decision, but she held her ground. Sally got on the very next flight out to see her mom.

When Sally arrived at the hospital, her mother said to her, "What took you so long?" Her mom died twelve hours later. The next day, Sally rang Rosemary and said, "You knew, didn't you? Thank you for not telling me, and thank you for getting me here."

Compassion is about caring for others and what they're going through and making things work. Sometimes what's good for the individual may look like it isn't what's best for the company, but in the long run it becomes that.

How do we become more compassionate leaders? By putting ourselves in someone else's position and asking ourselves how we'd like to be treated. We don't have to take on the problem or solve it, we just have to stay *in the moment*. We need to have the emotional courage to make the connection, feel the pain or hurt, and stay fully present. Listen. Be nonjudgmental. Guide when asked and be quiet when not asked. Practice empathetic listening and reflect on what the other person is feeling.

If you're the kind of leader who's uncomfortable around feelings, our best advice is to face the fear and feel anyway. With time, you'll experience more ease and calmness, and you'll have better, healthier relationships at home and at work.

A word about tears: Compassionate leaders recognize the full gamut of human emotions. When we're passionate about our work, it can be expressed in multiple ways, including crying, laughing, or getting angry. Anger is a call to action, which is why anger is often accompanied by a raised voice. There's real urgency expressed, a need to have something done differently, now. It's important. Unfortunately, most of us have learned to express anger only in the form of shouting, and that isn't something most of us enjoy or appreciate. Still, it seems to be acceptable that men shout, not women. And women aren't supposed to cry, either. There's no acceptable emotional outlet for women in the workplace. How unfair is that?

Susan Cain, *New York Times* bestselling author, explores the value of melancholy, sadness, and tears in her book *Bittersweet: How Sorrow and Longing Make Us Whole*: "We're taught from a very young age to scorn our own tears ('Crybaby!'), then to censure our sorrow for the rest of our lives. In a study of more than seventy thousand people, Harvard psychologist Dr. Susan David found that one-third of us judge ourselves for having 'negative' emotions such as sadness and grief."[30] Citing the

---

[30] Susan Cain, *Bittersweet: How Sorrow and Longing Make Us Whole* (New York: Crown, 2023), 6–12.

research of Dacher Keltner, Professor of Psychology at the University of California, Berkeley, and author of the book *Born to Be Good*, Cain goes on to express her belief that the compassionate instinct is also a fundamental aspect of the human success story—and one of the great powers of bittersweetness.

To become a balanced fearless leader, then, we must be compassionate and make room for all emotions, even those that have been shunned in the traditional leadership model. Tears of joy!

Attribute #4: Confidence
(Assurance, Certainty, Self-Worth, Self-Trust)

Confidence is defined as a belief that you can rely on someone or something, including yourself. To be confident, then, we must appreciate our own abilities and exemplify assurance. People who exude confidence tend to be more believable and appear to be more authentic. Men learn early on to embody this trait through their participation in sports and their interactions with their male friends.

Men and women tend to express confidence differently. Some men have mastered the ability to express full confidence regardless of experience or proof of ability. It's what drives men to apply for a job even if they can check off only three of the ten requirements asked for in the job description. Most women, on the other hand, feel compelled to be fully qualified and therefore won't apply for the job unless they can check off all ten requirements. This dichotomy explains how America elected a president who had zero experience in public service.

We believe that women and other people have been wrongly coached to "fake it 'til you make it." That's a nice idea, but confidence isn't something we can fake or manufacture. It comes from deep within and is conveyed through our energy, the very pores of our being.

What's more, women have been sold on the artificial condition called "imposter syndrome." The history of how this "syndrome" was identified is straight out of fiction. In a 2021 article published in *Harvard Business Review*, authors Ruchika Tulshyan and Jodi-Ann Burey explain the following:

"Imposter syndrome," or doubting your abilities and feeling like a fraud at work, is a diagnosis often given to women. But the fact that it's considered a diagnosis at all is problematic. The concept, whose development in the 1970s excluded the effects of systemic racism, classism, xenophobia, and other biases, took a universal feeling of discomfort, second-guessing, and mild anxiety in the workplace and pathologized it, especially for women. The answer to overcoming imposter syndrome is not to fix individuals but to create an environment that fosters different leadership styles and where diversity of racial, ethnic, and gender identities is viewed as just as professional as the current model.[31]

It's interesting to note that like many other limiting beliefs, imposter syndrome is now of interest among corporate male employees. We need to put an end to this fallacy before it becomes a corporate neurosis.

You are *not* an imposter. You are *not* defined by your self-doubt. You are real. Let's not speak of this again. Let's not put energy into something that doesn't serve us or support us as we move forward in our leadership journeys.

So what can men do to develop more confidence?

- Try new things. Fail faster.
- Be vulnerable and honest about what's in the way of your progress.
- Set aside your ego and embrace a beginner's mindset.
- Never again buy into the fallacy of imposter syndrome.

Women, on the other hand, persistently display what looks like a lack of confidence because they're wired to listen to criticism. This causes us to focus more on the negative than the positive, leading us and the people around us to wonder whether we can rely on one another.

So what can women do to shore up and sustain confidence?

---

[31] Ruchika Tulshyan and Jodi-Ann Burey, "Stop Telling Women They Have Imposter Syndrome," *Harvard Business Review*, February 22, 2021, https://hbr.org/2021/02/stop-telling-women-they-have-imposter-syndrome.

- Learn to talk about wins. Brag a bit.
- Internalize criticisms as suggestions for "possibilities" rather than "must-dos." (The latter is what guys do—it's their superpower.)
- Don't hesitate when giving an opinion. Speak affirmatively and firmly.
- Treat a mistake as a learning event. It happened. Fix it and move on.
- Never again buy into the fallacy of imposter syndrome.

A Glimpse

Susy embodies confidence in the loveliest of ways. At an early age, she learned to play a musical instrument. As she practiced, she kept getting better. Now, as she's going off to college, she says she has no worries about how she'll do; she knows, with certainty, that she'll succeed. Why? As she puts it, "I learned to fail and fail and fail with my clarinet. I just kept practicing until I got better. I apply that lesson to everything new I start. If I fail, I just practice until I get it right."

And that's all any of us need to do to build our confidence. So practice until you're confident.

Attribute #5: Resonance
(Vibrational Energy, Connection, Charisma, Inspiration)

When leaders develop resonance, they create environments that allow everyone to do and be their best. They ignite passion in others. They motivate and influence. Resonance, then, is a combination of tone and alignment between leaders and their teams. Tone includes passion, purpose, objective, problem-solving, and vocal awareness. When a team is on the same wavelength emotionally and mentally, they do things efficiently and effectively. People sometimes refer to these types of leaders as being "charismatic" when in fact they're being resonant. They understand that the source of their power is being who they truly are, not what they think other people want them to be.

Both men and women are capable of achieving and sustaining resonance. It's not a matter of personality, as extraverted and introverted leaders can equally resonate and inspire others. It's not about being outgoing or charismatic, either, and it's certainly not about being the center of attention. You don't need to be famous or bombastic to be a resonant leader. In fact that might work against you. Resonant leaders are humble and self-actualized. They're focused on others, not just themselves, and they have a vision and seek to be of service. This sends out vibrational energy that can't be manufactured or faked. People are naturally drawn to it.

How do you develop resonance? Start with knowing what you stand for. What's important to you? Do The Fearless Leader Manifesto exercise from chapter 3 and put into words your essence and beliefs. Then develop five to seven values that embody what's most important to you. You can borrow from the eight great attributes of fearless leadership in this chapter, or you can create your own. Whatever you choose, understand that these words describe not only your power but what will trigger you when these values are disrespected. As an example, one of Rosemary's values is wonder. She loves to explore, discover, and learn new things. Imagine what happens when she's around someone who has no curiosity, is set in their thinking, or is uninterested in exploring what works and what doesn't. She experiences ultimate frustration.

Once you develop more resonance, you'll begin to see the influence and potential you have to do more good in the world.

Attribute #6: Resilience
(Flexibility, Resourcefulness, Stamina, Grit, Hope)

Every leader, great and small, will be tested on what matters most to them, their vision, or their purpose—on what they hold dear. Most often these tests happen during circumstances that are less than ideal.

Resilient leaders can see a situation for what it truly is (and it's often harsh) and understand the need to remain firm yet flexible in the face of no agreement. This elasticity is what allows better solutions to present themselves. Like a muscle, resilience allows us, as individuals and as leaders, to bounce back from difficult situations and to deal with the stress and strain caused by today's ever-changing environment. In a nutshell, resilience allows us to bend without breaking, even in the most challenging situations.

According to Diane Coutu, the three cornerstones of resilience are:

1. Reality—being able to look at the harsh truth of a situation without losing hope.
2. Belief—deeply held values that allow one to search for meaning in hardship.
3. Improvisation—being able to make do with whatever is at hand; being inventive, using your ingenuity, and imagining possibilities.[32]

In her article "How Resilience Works," Coutu quotes Dean Becker, managing director of Adaptiv Learning Systems: "More than education, more than experience, more than training, a person's level of resilience will determine who succeeds and who fails. That's true in the cancer ward, it's true in the Olympics, and it's true in the boardroom."[33]

While both men and women (at any age) can embody the attribute of resilience, it tends to look more like resoluteness or determination for men. They often attempt to push through and "win" over obstacles. We see this in modern-day campaign slogans and speeches that contain phrases such as "We will never back down." Reminiscent of heroic battle cries, this expression of resilience is often described as grit. Fearless leaders should be mindful, as their egos and leadership shadows can cloud their judgment in these challenging situations. Grit must be tempered with restraint and humility.

---

[32] Diane Coutu, "How Resilience Works," Harvard Business Review, May 2002, https://hbr.org/2002/05/how-resilience-works.
[33] Coutu, "How Resilience Works."

Women tend to use harmony and flow to deal with difficult situations. This flow is what allows for the genius thinking of improvisation to manifest at the right time. Resilience allows leaders to thrive through intentionally exercising their diplomacy, grace, and mindfulness. These actions can make the difference between war and peace in the workplace, in the world, and in ourselves.

To cultivate the attribute of resilience, you must first find something that's meaningful to you (your values, personal vision, mission, or Manifesto), then develop a muscle around grounding yourself in reality about that circumstance. No sugarcoating, no excessive or blind optimism, no faking it until you make it, no denialism. If the reality is hard, you must strive to see it, accept it, and own it. Get rid of your limiting beliefs, then look for opportunities to improvise, including asking for help and using humor to cope. The answers will come, and you'll be ready, with your purpose as your shield and your perspective as your sword. Resilience will empower you to lead fearlessly toward more peaceful and prosperous outcomes—even in the face of hardship.

Attribute #7: Wisdom
(Good Judgment, Experience, Perception, Insight, Humility)

Wisdom is the ability to think analytically and to make powerful choices while understanding and taking into consideration the needs of others. Said in today's vernacular, it's the combination of analytical and emotional intelligence.

Some people have asked us what the difference is between wisdom and knowledge and whether wisdom naturally comes to people with experience and age. Here's what we know: 1) in life, knowledge and wisdom are not the same, and 2) aging is not a guarantee of wisdom. A person can spend decades acquiring information or skills yet never translate that knowledge into productive results. Wisdom is the ability to discern which aspects of that acquired knowledge are true, right, lasting, and applicable to your life and the world around you. It's about being able to turn that information into insights for the betterment of others, often as an expression of leadership. Combining wisdom and leadership elevates and empowers both leaders and their followers.

Strategy consultant and university educator Chris Ellis proposes a simple definition for wisdom in the context of leadership. In his article "The Pillars of Leadership Wisdom," Ellis writes, "Leadership wisdom is the combined use of awareness, experience, and insight to set direction, empower people, ensure well-being, and guide activity to achieve lasting results . . . Leadership wisdom develops from active engagement, objective observation, and deep reflection."[34] As the authors of this book, we believe that the nature of leadership is evolving and must continue to evolve in conscious, gender-neutral ways.

A conscious leader creates an environment of fun, curiosity, and accountability around making mistakes. When we become better as a result of our experiences, we can incorporate the wisdom of the moment into our being. We become more conscious, more aware, and those around us are enlivened.

How do we become wiser? Begin by embodying the masculine trait of knowing with the feminine trait of understanding. Both sexes need to incorporate this embodiment. Here are some ways to cultivate wisdom:

- Embrace new things. Actively seek out different experiences.
- Change your perspective from "mistakes" to "learning opportunities."
- Seek first to understand. If only for a moment, walk a mile in someone else's shoes.
- Choose growth over fear. Do what's right over what's easy, safe, or popular.

Gaining wisdom is a valuable leadership attribute open to all people at any age. But it requires significant work, including reflection, experience, curiosity, and vulnerability. Becoming wise is a very

---

[34] Chris Ellis, "The Pillars of Leadership Wisdom," University of Chicago | Center for Practical Wisdom, July 6, 2020, https://wisdomcenter.uchicago.edu/news/discussions/pillars-leadership-wisdom.

personal quest that becomes part of your leadership journey when you choose to embrace it.

Attribute #8: Humor
(Ease, Lightness, Perspective, Reframing, Relief)

Humor is a desirable trait in leaders. It can be used to create connections, reduce stress, relieve workplace pressure, and produce well-being and joy in a group situation. But when it comes to leadership humor, there's no one-size-fits-all model.

Men use humor to bond and create connections with other guys. This often takes the form of levity, joking, and kidding around. Practical jokes, making fun of others, and off-color or crude comments are generally acceptable between guys. We raise them to "horse around." Though women sometimes think it is, especially when it's directed at them, men's intention with their humor usually isn't to belittle people.

In contrast, most women tend to express humor through emotional storytelling. They generally practice a more inclusive and affiliative style of humor. Women make jokes to create "a lightness of being" and bring safety and connection to a situation. When men try to do that, they often come off as insensitive and brutish. It ends up feeling like gallows humor[35] (also known as dark humor), and it kills connection, understanding, and bonding lightning fast.

It's important to note that women should avoid employing locker-room-style humor with men. We often fail at this because we don't understand its purpose or how to deliver it safely. Coauthor Kathy learned this lesson the hard way (although looking back now, it's humorous).

---

[35] Jafar Al-Mondhiry et al., "Gallows Humor," October 30, 2019, in *At the Bedside*, produced by Core IM, podcast, MP3 audio, 47:04, https://www.coreimpodcast.com/2019/10/30/gallows-humor/.

A Glimpse

Kathy was working in the medical device industry in the early 1990s when she first learned there were different rules around humor at work for men and women. She had a colleague named Dan who could captivate the executive team during his presentations. She thought if she could be funny like Dan, the executive team would be eating out of her hands too.

Kathy pushed her humor boundaries, and it was a disaster. An epic failure. The executive team just sat there in silence with expressionless faces. They were in shock. That's when Kathy determined that her personal brand didn't include moving to the edges of humor or using profanity like the guys. What she didn't realize was that she was using male humor incorrectly, and it landed like an insult.

According to international speaker, author, and neurohumorist Karyn Buxman, humor is a learnable, teachable skill. She recommends that people become students of humor, tune into humor, and look for it in everyday life: "Good leaders don't leave humor to chance. They weave it in intentionally."[36] Buxman also recommends a moderate use of self-effacing humor that focuses on our actions rather than ourselves. This type of humor shows our vulnerability, humility, humanity, and courage. She strongly recommends that we, especially women, avoid self-deprecating humor, the kind used to make fun of ourselves as people, because it positions us as small and flawed. In short, it's okay to laugh about our mistakes, but we should never laugh our self-worth away.

Margaret Cho, a renowned comedian, actor, artist, and activist, reminds us of the saving grace of humor: "It's good to be able to laugh at yourself and the problems you face in life. A sense of humor can save you."[37]

---

[36] Karyn Buxman, interview with Kathy McAfee, January 13, 2023.
[37] Peter Gaston, "Exclusive: Margaret Cho Teams with Tegan & Sara!" SPIN, August 2, 2010, https://www.spin.com/2010/08/exclusive-margaret-cho-teams-tegan-sara/.

There are five things we can do to cultivate humor as one of our leadership attributes:

1. Take an improvisational class to practice experiencing how to be more spontaneous. Learning how to create a lead-in and a handoff builds a bridge to a new point of view and a new action.
2. Train ourselves to "see the funny" by recording in a humor journal all the funny things we notice and enjoy each day.
3. Don't take ourselves too seriously. Lighten up. Be the first to laugh at our mistakes and human foibles. Give ourselves permission to smile and chuckle more often. Laugh out loud several times a day.
4. Learn to release the tension and constriction in our bodies (especially our hands) and on our faces (especially our tongues). Less grinding, more fun.
5. Make the commitment to be impeccable with our humor. Never use humor as a social weapon. Model positive, healthy, good humor only.

* * * * *

What's Next?

In the next chapter, we ask for your help to reinvent a new kind of leader, to reimagine a different narrative and an altered storyline for the heroine's journey. The world we envision is one in which women can be unencumbered and uber-successful simply by embracing their full and true nature. Women should no longer be forced to disconnect and cast off their feminine qualities and innate abilities. When we're successful in achieving this mission, we'll have an empowering new storyline—a new reality for our Shero's Journey to share with future generations of girls and women, and indeed all people.

CHAPTER 5

Reinventing Leadership

You are stronger than you believe. You have greater power than you know.
~Antiope to Diana, Wonder Woman (2017)

As humans we learn, recall, and change best through storytelling. Marketing and advertising firms understand that the best way to attract clients (and sell services) is by quickly and succinctly telling a story that leads the audience who hears the message to arrive at the desired conclusion. Storytelling is used everywhere, from our apps to the stories we tell our young children, the movies we watch, and even this book. All these conduits are trying to teach us by helping us change how we think about ourselves. Storytelling shapes our journeys toward becoming leaders and frames our experiences from failures to wins, from shortcomings to talents, and from barriers to breakthroughs.

Movies are very successful at using certain tools to tell their stories for the desired effect. In the documentary *The Hero's Journey: The World of Joseph Campbell*,[38] Campbell discusses how movies have well-defined hero templates with a specific series of events, usually involving a hero who leaves the comfort of his community, goes on an

---

[38] *The Hero's Journey: The World of Joseph Campbell*, directed by Janelle Balnicke and David Kennard (1987; Hudson, OH: Acorn Media, 2012), DVD.

adventure to overcome an obstacle or enemy, and returns home victorious, changed, and transformed. The hero is then acknowledged as a leader by his community. That template works great for men but not so much for women. The heroine's journey, or becoming a "spiritual warrior"[39] as Maureen Murdock calls it, requires women to first separate from community and release their femininity and embrace the masculine warrior qualities. Then they must reintegrate their feminine qualities. But the movies aren't showing us how to do that. No role models. No road maps. No evidence of safe passage. We need something for us.

That's what we want to provide right here, right now. We want to create the Shero's Journey: a journey all people can take that integrates the best of both masculine and feminine leadership traits to produce a holistic leader who inspires all of us to be better and do better; a whole leader who can model how to embody masculine power traits with collaborative, inclusive feminine traits; a fearless leader who's respected regardless of gender.

Resolving Problems

From the survey we discussed in chapter 1, we learned that there are four primary barriers women face today when it comes to being recognized as a leader in the workplace. If left unresolved, these barriers can become lasting problems for women. Let's unpack these four barriers and share problem-solving tips, examples, and motivators to help you succeed on your Shero's Journey.

Problem #1: Not Having a Mentor

According to our survey, having a mentor is the most important factor needed to become a leader and to be recognized as a leader at any age. Successful businessmen understand the value of mentors, and up-and-coming male leaders have mentors seek them out. Many

---

[39] Murdock, The Heroine's Journey, 11.

women, however, consistently insist on climbing the ladder of success without support. Without help.

Most successful women point to the support they needed to win. Consider these six successful female leaders, all who went on the record with *Huffington Post* to acknowledge their male mentors: Tracy Britt, Sheryl Sandberg, Ursula Burns, Tina Fey, Condoleezza Rice, and Indra Nooyi.[40] We'd also add our names to the list of successful women leaders who've benefited from having male mentors during our Shero's Journeys. We had doors opened for us (by men for the most part) that otherwise would've been out of our reach. Why not you?

As a Vistage Chair, coauthor Rosemary found it very difficult to add women to her groups. When interviewed, the women consistently said, "Why do I need a peer group? I can do this on my own." Sure you can, but what cost in time and money are you willing to expend to figure it out on your own? Mentors and peers can offer suggestions and open doors to the right partners and pathways to accelerate your growth.

So what *is* a mentor anyway? The *Oxford English Dictionary* defines it as "a person who acts as guide and adviser to another person, esp. one who is younger and less experienced; a person who offers support and guidance to another; an experienced and trusted counsellor or friend."[41] Most people think a mentor is primarily a teacher. While, yes, mentors teach, advise, and share their perspectives and wisdom, they also open the right doors to help advance our careers. They are people who can put in the right word to ease a promotion or advancement. Some people refer to this as a sponsor. For purposes of this book, we integrate the sponsor role into the mentor role.

Of course, a mentor can help smooth out the rough edges in a person's growth and development as a leader through storytelling, observation, and advice. But that's the icing on the cake. The cake itself

---

[40] Nina Bahadur, "6 Women Who Credit Their Male Mentors with Helping Them Find Success," HuffPost, last modified December 6, 2017, https://www.huffpost.com/entry/women-mentored-by-men-gender-matter_n_3894659.

[41] *Oxford English Dictionary*, 2nd ed. (Oxford: Oxford University Press, 2004), s.v. "mentor (n.)."

is the influence and access. Having someone open the right doors at the right times is a game-changer. Climbing the corporate ladder all on your own with no mentor, no outside help, is a painstaking and slow process that only the most persistent of souls can accomplish. This leaves many good women leaders floundering on the sidelines hoping to be noticed, seen; hoping that her achievements will speak for themselves, as our moms tell us. Meanwhile, men are racing ahead in their careers with the help of their mentors.

No matter how smart or successful you think you can become, finding a mentor makes it so much easier (and faster) to achieve. As seasoned businesswomen, and with the scars to prove it, we coauthors believe this wholeheartedly. Then what's in our way? Is it that there aren't enough women in mentorship positions? Perhaps. Not enough women hold executive roles these days. But we argue that *all* women have the potential to be excellent mentors and door-openers for other women. Is it that women are just too darn independent, wanting to prove that they can do it without anyone's help? Perhaps. As women we can be a bit too prideful. Many of us don't want to ask men for help, and others haven't had much luck getting help from women either. So we choose to go it alone, without the aid of a mentor. Big mistake.

To become fearless female leaders, we must start the process of finding a mentor as soon as possible. The first step is admitting we want one. We then need to identify how a mentor could help us, being clear where we want their help (training, opening doors, bringing new opportunities to you), and go find the person (or several persons) who best fits the bill. And, for heaven's sake, let's learn to become mentors ourselves.

A word about pride: It's good to feel proud of our accomplishments. In fact, in the previous chapter we gave you permission to brag a bit about your successes. Women don't do enough bragging, usually for fear it will morph into pride, arrogance, or feelings of superiority. Pride can quickly turn reasonable self-esteem and confidence into delusional invincibility and hubris. Getting help from others not only accelerates and enhances our achievement but helps us remain humble—the antidote for arrogance.

We also know women who reject mentoring outright. They say things like, "I have it handled" or "I'm self-taught." Some women pass on their disregard for mentoring by advising others, "Stop asking people to mentor you." These negative attitudes toward mentoring (likely stemming from their leadership shadows) cost them a lot in support and networking. Worse yet, they cause women to miss out on opportunities to help others in their Shero's Journeys.

Mentoring comes to a dead end with these kinds of leaders. Don't be one of them. Always pay it forward by actively mentoring others. (And, what the heck, develop the healthy habits of humility and gratitude while you're at it.)

> **A Glimpse**
>
> Early in coauthor Rosemary's career, she had a female boss we'll call Alice. Naively, Rosemary thought Alice would want to help advance Rosemary's career. She couldn't have been more wrong. When Rosemary asked for mentorship and support, Alice said, "Why should I help you? I had to work my ass off to get this position. You're on your own." Unbeknownst to Alice, Rosemary had already gone to the CEO and asked why it was that Alice, who was the controller of the company, wasn't included in the manager meetings when the former controller (a man) had been. Alice was immediately instated into the management group. But she was unwilling to use her influence and support to help Rosemary rise in the ranks. Oh dear.

Is it that with everything we're juggling we just don't have the time to even think to look for a mentor, much less define what a good mentor is? Is it that we think we have to be superwomen, do it all, and do it better than anyone else? Do we think we can't ask anyone for help or admit we might need help? Do we really have to do it all alone? Imagine how we might benefit if we only had the courage to seek out and secure a good mentor or two in our professional lives.

To speed your process of identifying and cultivating mentors, here's a list of important attributes your mentor needs to possess:

- An excellent reputation in your industry
- Expertise in your industry
- Skip-level leadership (they aren't currently your direct manager)
- A willingness to advocate for you
- A circle of influence that contains the best of the best people and is open to you; they are "influential mavens" (à la Malcolm Gladwell's book *The Tipping Point*)[42]
- No qualms or issues about promoting women
- An affinity toward you
- A personality you can work with

And here is what's *not* important in a mentor:

- Their sex or identity
- Their title
- Where (or if) they work (they don't have to work at your company; often they're retired)

Now that you have the criteria, your objective is to find at least six people who could become your mentor. Look at your company and your industry to identify as many people as you can who fit your bill. Assess peer groups, your friend circles, your networking circles (like bankers, CPAs, and attorneys), and the thought leaders of your industry. Make a list and start asking whether they'd be willing to support you. Yes, you have to ask these important, influential people whether they'll become your mentor, and sometimes they'll say no. Be fearless and keep seeking out mentors.

Why six people? These are cherished relationships that take time to nurture and support, which is why having more than six is difficult to maintain. Yes, you need to talk to them every month. These are people

---

[42] Malcolm Gladwell, *The Tipping Point: How Little Things Can Make a Big Difference* (New York: Back Bay Books, 2002), 30–88.

you're invested in and who are willing to be or are invested in your success. Staying in touch is essential.

Once you get high enough in a corporate environment, you can pay it forward by becoming a mentor yourself. There are many benefits to becoming a mentor. According to Samantha Surillo, managing director and executive coach with Courtex Performance, LLC, the sheer act of mentoring may help individuals develop *leader identity*, which is defined as whether and how you think of yourself as a leader, and *leader self-efficacy*, which is defined as confidence in your ability to perform as a leader and engage in leadership behaviors. These two aspects are essential to helping individuals continue to emerge and grow as leaders and self-actualized human beings.[43]

In short, by mentoring others you're also helping yourself grow, develop, and evolve. In turn, this can become a positive influence on your own Shero's Journey.

Problem #2: No Flexibility at Work or Support at Home

Having the support at home and the flexibility at work to handle our home life issues is essential to succeeding at work. Back in the day, men had wives to take care of all the details they didn't have time (or interest) to handle. To have a big, successful career, it's essential to have support around the mundane tasks. Many women who have big careers chose spouses who either stayed at home to tend to the family or had jobs that were secondary to their careers. This meant that the man's career was more flexible or wasn't as high a priority, so he could quit his job to follow his wife's career. It was a straight-up role reversal of the traditional male playbook. Women said, "This is how men succeed, so I will follow their example."

---

[43] Samantha Surillo, "Successful Mentor Programs: Demystifying the Key Benefits & Elements," Courtex Performance, November 2022, https://www.courtexperformance.com/whitepaper.

A Glimpse

Coauthor Kathy's husband, Byron, took the bold and loving step to assume a secondary role so that her career could take off and lead them both to some amazing places. When Kathy was offered an incredible career-making position in Europe, Byron quit his job and followed her. They enjoyed three full years working and living in England. He enrolled in an MBA program, which gave him both intellectual stimulation and the flexibility they needed as a couple. When some of the male executives in Kathy's firm questioned whether Byron was really "okay" with her being the primary breadwinner and not working, she said, "Of course. Doesn't your spouse do the same for you?"

There doesn't have to be only one person in a relationship who's successful. Interesting things can happen when we expand our thinking about roles and responsibilities at work and at home. Extraordinary things can occur when we don't assume that the woman must take care of the home and kids first and her career second or that the husband must give up his career for his wife to be successful. Many men today want to be integrated into their children's lives. They understand firsthand what it feels like to not have a dad around or to have a single mom juggling both work and home. Many women have realized that trying to be a supermom means they don't get to enjoy being a mom. A new model for success is being called forth.

To cultivate flexibility and support, the first thing we need to do is change our thinking that males must be the primary breadwinners in the family. We must also change our thinking that females are primarily responsible for caregiving and maintaining the household. This is an outdated statistic, an old concept. Despite the lingering, annoying, unfair, and terribly unjust wage gap, women are earners too. Rather than assigning tasks by gender, why not consider assigning household and family duties by preference? Who's better at it? Who enjoys it more? Who's better qualified to perform the task?

Next, create a long list of all the things that need to be done to support the household, including maintaining vehicles, taking out the trash, doing the dishes, taking the kids or pets to the doctor . . . you get the idea. Then determine who's going to do what. This can be done on a rotating schedule. It can also be that neither partner likes the task, in which case you can hire someone to support it, even a neighbor's kid. Get creative and consider other resources.

Remember, you don't have to do everything by yourself. Your success team at home should be bigger than "me, myself, and I." You might also have to think outside the box when it comes to higher-level tasks and those that require expertise. Consider hiring a virtual personal assistant and making arrangements at work to allow for more flexibility with your start and end times.

A Glimpse

Coauthor Rosemary had a staff accountant working for her named Sasha, who was a single mom. Sasha needed time off every day when school ended to take her son to an aftercare program at 2:30 p.m. They agreed she'd take her lunch hour at that time because the firm was inflexible about taking additional time off. If Sasha needed to work late, she'd bring her son in at 6:00 p.m. when most of the other staff were gone. Without that kind of flexibility, Sasha couldn't have worked at this company nor supported her family. And Rosemary would've lost one of the best employees she had.

The true winner was Sasha's son. He got to spend more time with his mom and feel like he mattered. This was likely his first on-the-job training as a future leader: witnessing what workplace flexibility looks and feels like.

The bottom line is that flexibility and support help everyone, from family units and individuals within the family to employers and communities. Look for where you can ask for support and where your company can provide flexibility.[44] Both support and flexibility are essential conditions for the new Shero's Journey to succeed. Without them, the Shero is left on their own to flounder and face unnecessary suffering on their way to transformation. Let's help our fellow Sheroes by giving them the flexibility and support they require to succeed and lead.

Problem #3: Lack of Confidence

According to our survey, lack of confidence is a persistent problem that permeates a woman's career. Given the lack of support they get at home and the lack of flexibility they have in the workplace, however, is it really a lack of confidence in their abilities, or is it a lack of confidence in the system to support their dreams and visions?

When women feel they have to prove themselves, it can trigger them to try to do everything by themselves. But being a lone wolf can lead to an erosion of confidence. We stop trusting or relying on others even when we need them the most. That erosion can then leak over to the confidence and trust we have in ourselves, and that's where the true danger to a woman's confidence lies.

In an article she wrote for O, The Oprah Magazine, journalist and author Aimee Lee Ball says this:

> Why is it that some people, the Donald Trumps of the world, seem to believe only the best about themselves, while others—perhaps especially women, perhaps especially young women—seize on the most self-critical thoughts they can come up with? "It turns out there's an area of your brain that's assigned the task of negative thinking," says Louann Brizendine, MD, a neuropsychiatrist at the University of California, San Francisco, and the author of The Female Brain. "It's judgmental. It says, 'I'm too fat' or 'I'm too old.' It's a barometer of every social interaction you have. It goes on red alert when the feedback you're getting from other people isn't going well." This worrywart part of the brain is the anterior cingulate cortex. In women, it's actually larger and more influential, as is the brain circuitry for observing

---

[44] At the back of this book, we provide many resources to help you do this, including a link to Untapped Potential, Inc. and their Flexreturn program.

emotions in others. "The reason we think females have more emotional sensitivity," says Brizendine, "is that we've been built to be immediately responsive to the needs of a nonverbal infant. That can be both a good thing and a bad thing."[45]

In other words, women are biologically built to be more self-critical. Confidence, then, is a learned experience. It might help if we looked at it from a slightly different perspective.

Confidence is generally defined as an appreciation of someone's abilities and qualities. But it's more than that. It's also having the expectation that others will have our backs and believe in us. You know how good you are. You know your skills and abilities and what you're capable of. But do you trust that others will have your back when you need it most? Do you trust yourself? Trust, self-awareness, and lived experience are the underpinnings of sustainable self-confidence. When you come to know and trust yourself and others, you'll be able to lead more authentically.

Some people think you can fake it until you make it, but we disagree. We've found in our work with fearless leaders that true confidence cannot be manufactured or purchased; it must be organically cultivated and nurtured. True confidence means being vulnerable, not needy or helpless. It means having the courage to expose our weaknesses and fears, knowing that by facing them our potential for growth increases. Being vulnerable opens us to attack where we're weakest, but it also helps us shore up those areas. Being vulnerable takes courage, and it can become your superpower.

On your Shero's Journey, your confidence will ebb and flow. That's only natural because you'll face tasks and trials that are new, scary, and difficult. With each step forward, your confidence will grow and you'll begin to transform. Remember to keep taking that next step.

---

[45] Aimee Lee Ball, "Women and the Negativity Receptor," Oprah.com, accessed August 17, 2023, https://www.oprah.com/omagazine/why-women-have-low-self-esteem-how-to-feel-more-confident/all.

Problem #4: Ageism

Ageism is a problem for both men and women in the beginning of their careers when they are deemed "too young" or "too inexperienced." At the end of their careers (usually when they're in their fifties or sixties), they can also feel like there's some prejudice. Young folks think that older folks aren't embracing new technology fast enough and thus need to be replaced like an obsolete landline. Older professionals feel that younger generation professionals are seeking rapid advancement without putting in the time and effort to earn it. This is an argument not worth having. Every generation criticizes the one that follows, and vice versa.

The real problem is that we think the need for innovative thinking and new design—what young people have in abundance—is the same as the need for strategic thinking and problem-solving—what older people have cultivated with experience. It isn't. Both innovation and strategy are needed, and both younger and older professionals are needed.

Though most people experience ageism at the beginning and end of their careers, what's different for women is the middle years. It seems that many managers consider a woman in child-bearing years to also be a liability because at any moment she could leave to have kids. This isn't true for men. Starting and having a family doesn't seem to be a liability for a man. With all the progress made in the last fifty years, these issues are still impeding women's career advancement.

A Glimpse

Wendy had just celebrated her sixty-sixth birthday when the global pandemic erupted. Like millions of other people, she was laid off from her full-time job. She was no stranger to disruptions in her career and life, as she had successfully navigated the challenges of being divorced and raising her two kids as a single mother. Her career was in corporate training and development, and she experienced layoffs every time

> there was an economic downturn. But this time, she knew that finding another job was going to be much more difficult. Her intuition told her it was her age and the pandemic that would make this transition much more challenging.
>
> Wendy wasn't ready to be done. She knew she wanted to feel relevant, like she still mattered, and that she could still make a difference. She revamped her brand, reconnected with her purpose, and completed The Fearless Leader program. Wendy is now a boomer transition coach, the successful host of the *Hey, Boomer!* podcast and live show, and a thought leader in the pro-aging movement. She inspires adults in their next acts of life to find new beginnings, confront endings, and transition into who they want to be. Just like C. S. Lewis, Wendy believes that "You are never too old to set another goal or dream a new dream."

Though women should be relevant at any age, it starts to feel like there's no "right" time in a woman's career to advance it. When a woman in the 1960s or 1970s took on a career, she often gave up having children. It was an either/or world. Many women didn't want to give up being a mom, so in the 1980s they took on the persona of a superwoman doing it all: full-time mother, full-time wife, full-time career. Exhausting. Unsustainable. Today, many women delay starting a family, and many expect more engagement from their spouse in child rearing. But is that enough?

Balancing work and family is one of the most difficult trials women face on their Shero's Journeys. Many people have tried to spin the problem with a clever rewording like "work–life fit," "work–life harmony," or "work–life integration." But the root cause of the problem hasn't gone away. At its core remains a significant deficit of flexibility and support: not enough time, not enough flexibility, not enough help, not enough support. Other countries have cracked the code on this perennial workplace problem. Why not Corporate America? Until all people embrace the concept that raising children is a societal matter rather than a female obligation, women will continue to bear the brunt of balancing family and career.

Perhaps the sidekick a woman needs to accompany her on her Shero's Journey could be a nanny, a free on-site daycare, a personal chef and housekeeper, or a personal assistant. Or maybe it's an understanding boss or a partner at home. Imagine what you could do with that kind of flexibility and support at any age.

Changing the Journey

In summary, we can and must change how the Shero's Journey plays out in modern society. It's more than folklore. It's the storyline of our collective lives. But we don't have to continue to rerun the same old story. It's time to make the changes necessary for taking a different journey, like the one illustrated at the end of this chapter by Megan L. Robinson, a graduate of The Fearless Leader program.

The choice before all of us is this: Do I return to what I know, or do I choose the road less traveled? By continuing the journey and facing the inner challenge, you'll emerge as a thriving, balanced, holistic leader, returning home celebrated and revered by your community of supporters.

*****

In part 3, we introduce you to real women who've faced insurmountable odds with fearlessness. Their stories, or "fearless leader moments" as we like to call them, highlight how the eight great attributes of fearless leadership can be applied to real world situations. Like these women, you too can overcome barriers and become a more fearless leader of your life, career, and business. Read on.

The Shero's Journey

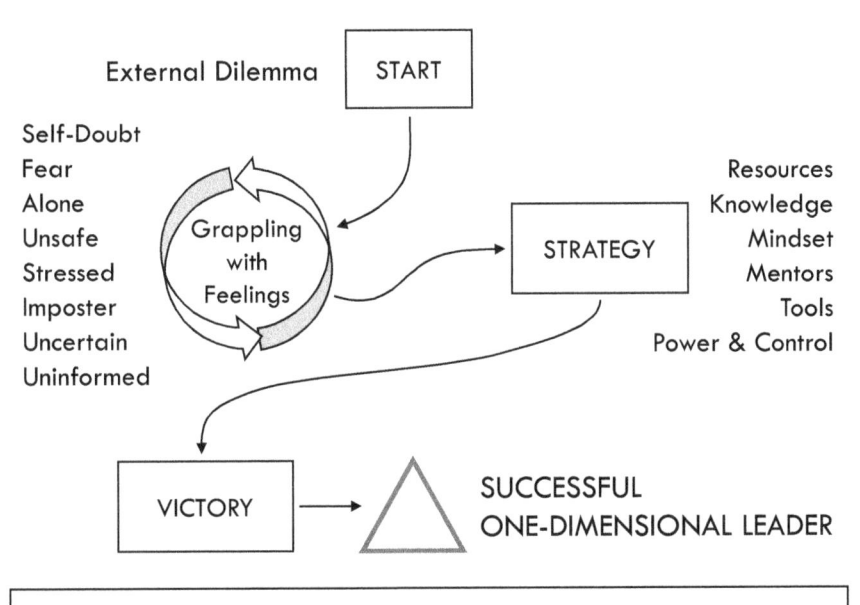

External Dilemma — START

Self-Doubt
Fear
Alone
Unsafe
Stressed
Imposter
Uncertain
Uninformed

Grappling with Feelings

STRATEGY

Resources
Knowledge
Mindset
Mentors
Tools
Power & Control

VICTORY → SUCCESSFUL ONE-DIMENSIONAL LEADER

UNCOVERING THE TREASURE

Internal Impasse — EXPLORE

Rejection
Failure
Betrayal
Shadow
Ego
Identity
Limiting Belief

FEARS & BLOCKS

INTEGRATE

Trust
Clarity
Values
Alignment
Team
Mentoring
Self-Actualization

FINISH! → THRIVING BALANCED, HOLISTIC LEADER

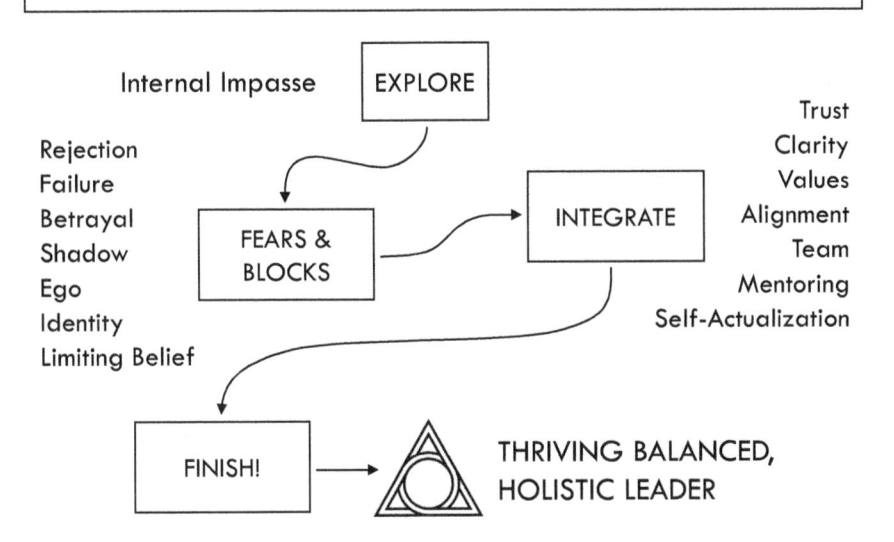

Illustration by Megan L. Robinson

Fear less and LEAD MORE

Download two great resources:
1) Shero's Journey Guidebook by Megan L. Robinson; 2) the article *"Successful Mentor Programs"* by Samantha Surillo

Access bonus gifts here:
fearlessleaderbooks.com/bonuses

PART 3

EMPOWERING ROLE MODELS:

Following Fearless Footsteps

CHAPTER 6

Focusing on What's Most Important

Don't ignore the pain. Give it purpose. Use it.
~Amanda Gorman

To lead means that we must first focus on what's most important, then make new choices. Doing that will define who we are and how much joy we experience. Below are two stories of women who dared to stay true to what was most important amid some challenging circumstances. Rather than staying stuck in the unjustness and unfairness of their situation, they dared to make a difference. They paved the way for many other fearless leaders to serve and soar to new heights.

Sylvia Whitlock
Fearless in the Face of Discrimination

"I don't think you wrote it. In fact, you couldn't have written that yourself," explained the teacher. "That's why I gave you a C."

The young woman, a college freshman, just stood there in disbelief. She'd been raised by her grandmother not to argue with her elders, so she remained silent as this college teacher judged her wrongly.

Sylvia had been so excited about the assignment to write an essay on the poem "On His Blindness" by John Milton, which describes the struggles that Milton faced after he lost his eyesight and how he used his personal experience to explore his faith and find anew his purpose.[46] Little did she know that she too would have to take a similar journey.

As a high school student in Jamaica, Sylvia had studied Milton's poem extensively. If the teacher had asked her to, Sylvia could've recited the sonnet from memory right then and there. But she was so shocked and confused by this unexpected moment that she didn't think to defend herself or her work. She humbly walked out of the teacher's office with her brilliant essay in hand and the teacher's condescending grade splashed in red ink on the front page. It just as well might've said, "Rejected."

"Welcome to the big city," said her mother when Sylvia returned home to their apartment and explained what had happened that afternoon in the teacher's office. "No one's going to give a Black girl a free ride. You must be twice as good as the rest of them. And you must be tough. You can't let this destroy you or make you lose your faith in yourself."

It was 1951, and America was deep in the throes of the Civil Rights Movement. All over the country, local and state mandates known as Jim Crow Laws were marginalizing African Americans, denying them the right to vote, hold jobs, get an education, or pursue other opportunities. Even in a sophisticated place like New York City, equal rights and equal treatment were, well, not equal.

Although Sylvia was born in New York City, she didn't have a lot of memories of the place. When she was five years old, her mother, a single mom and registered nurse, sent Sylvia and her brother to Jamaica

---

[46] Peter G. Epps, "10 Greatest Poems Written by John Milton," Society of Classical Poets, November 7, 2017, https://classicalpoets.org/2017/11/07/10-greatest-poems-written-by-john-milton/.

to go to school and live with their grandmother. It was a difficult decision, but she knew her children would face far less discrimination and have better educational opportunities than they would if they stayed in America during their primary and secondary school years. In hindsight, her fearless decision changed everything for her children.

So, this female student, a Black girl with a Bronx/Caribbean accent, set aside her pride and sadness and committed to studying even harder. She needed to do well to maintain her scholarship and graduate from Hunter College, a public college located in the heart of New York City. More than anything, Sylvia wanted to make her grandmother and her mother proud of her.

But for some reason, this intelligent and hardworking student who had always thrived in school was now struggling to get the kind of grades she knew she was capable of. Her grade point average started to erode, which put her in a precarious position with her scholarship. Suddenly, she was at risk of not being able to fulfill the academic requirements for graduation. Fortunately, the college provided her with a classroom supervisor until her grades improved.

Rather than focusing on the unfairness of her situation, Sylvia kept focusing on what her mother and her grandmother said was most important: education was the key to opportunity. She went on to graduate on time from Hunter College with a bachelor's degree in psychology and begin a career in teaching. She then earned a master's degree in education, which allowed her to advance in her professional field.

A true believer in the power of education, Sylvia earned her PhD in education at the age of forty-three. It was then that she received an unexpected letter from Hunter College congratulating her on her distinguished career and academic achievements. The letter explained that young Sylvia had been one of ten Black girls at Hunter College who were allowed to continue attending classes while on probation until their grades and performance improved. She never knew about these other girls. She thought she was the only one who was struggling and not meeting expectations. It turned out that all ten girls went on to earn advanced degrees.

Looking back on this college experience some sixty-six years later, Sylvia has this advice for other young people, especially people of color who may be facing similar situations: "Plot the course. Make a plan for where you want to go in your life. Believe in yourself. Don't be deterred by others. Do the hard work. Invest in yourself through education. You can get where you want to go if you just keep moving."

Clearly, Sylvia's attributes of boldness, confidence, and resilience got her through many barriers in her educational life and career. She overcame injustice and unfairness to do great things—not only for herself but for others. She learned to trust her intuition, share her wisdom, and develop a resonance in her leadership style that had people wanting to follow her. Yet her leadership continued to be challenged.

In 1976, driven by her love of serving the community, Sylvia joined the local Rotary Club in Duarte, California. Being of service was an important part of Sylvia's personal leadership brand. Ten years later, she was elected president and became the very first female ever to serve as president of a Rotary Club. All was good until "the letter" came.

Sylvia and others in her club were quite shocked to receive notification from Rotary International that women weren't allowed to be members. Only men were allowed membership, and only men could be presidents and officers. But unlike the awkward moment of subservience in the teacher's office in 1951, this time Sylvia chose to take action. She spoke up. She asked for help. She got others to join her in addressing this problem, and she enrolled others to help her right this wrong. This time she would not accept the decree. This time she would not go it alone.

Together, her team challenged the status quo. They defended it all the way to the US Supreme Court. On May 4, 1987, after an eleven-year legal battle, the highest court in the land ruled that Rotary Clubs may not exclude women from membership based on gender.[47] Shortly thereafter, the Rotary Organization issued a policy statement that any Rotary Club in the US can admit qualified women into membership.

It turns out that what appeared to be a membership issue was really a civil rights issue. And they had won it. They proved that women, too, can be of service and lead effectively. Today, Rotary Clubs all over the

---

[47] *Rotary Int'l v. Rotary Club of Duarte*, 481 U.S. 537 (1987), https://supreme.justia.com/cases/federal/us/481/537/.

US and in most countries around the world are made up of a diverse mix of members—men and women; Black and White; young and old; straight and gay; cisgender, transgender, or nonbinary; Christians and people of other faiths; and more—all working together to make the world a better place for others.

Sylvia frames this event in this way: "I didn't earn this or do anything special, but I did stick with it, and I represented it with integrity. Sometimes that's the only thing, and the most important thing, you can do."

And the cherry on top of this fearless leader story is that Sylvia received notification in 2020 from Hunter College that they put her on their distinguished alumni Wall of Fame. And in 2022, Rotary International voted to create the Sylvia Whitlock Leadership Award, honoring one Rotary member each year who has worked to advance women in Rotary. At long last, Sylvia is being celebrated and honored upon returning victorious from her Shero's Journey.

Complaining about how unfairly she was being treated (and she was) wouldn't have advanced Sylvia's education, her career, or her many accomplishments. By focusing on what was most important to her (her values), Sylvia was able to affect change at the highest level.

Jane (Ballard) Dyer
Fearless in the Face of Sexism

The time had come to cast the final vote. Days of haggling and debating had preceded this event. The team of sixty airmen were ready to cast their votes on the top five team goals. This vote would set the tone and tenor for their class at the US Air Force's undergraduate pilot training program in Del Rio, Texas. These hand-selected, high-potential future pilots had banded together to create the context in which they would achieve their greatest dream: to fly for the United States Air Force.

The energy in the room was thick with bravado. Back slapping, jeering, and choice words were loudly shared to bring the vote home. There was only one dissenting vote. But no one cared about that. After all, Jane was a woman, and she didn't belong here anyway. And the final vote would go down as the official five goals of Class 82-05:

1. Push the limits of aviation capability.
2. Excel in all physical tests and demands.
3. Meet all requirements for pilot knowledge, judgment, skill in critical flight, and ground tasks.
4. No man left behind.
5. No woman shall graduate from this class.

Yup. They all (but Jane) voted to make sure that she wouldn't graduate. Deflated and angry, she asked herself, *How the hell could this have taken place? How could the US Air Force permit this kind of discrimination and sexism to stand? What have I gotten myself into?*

As she sat at the table, alone in the room, her mind cast back to a simpler time. Her father, a remarkable man, had infused in her the courage, dignity, and deep belief that girls could do anything boys could do. The sixth child of a family of eight siblings, Jane learned about responsibility early on. "I wasn't supposed to be the most responsible, but I am," Jane reflects.

Her father was raised on a farm with a large family, and he was committed to building a better life than he had growing up. He went to college and graduated from the prestigious Clemson University with a degree in mechanical engineering. He then went on to the Army Air Corps and was an active-duty serviceman in the Pacific during World War II. During that mission, he helped build infrastructure, including runways. He built tent communities for the servicemen and had the ingenious idea to fight off the Pacific deluge of rain by pouring a concrete floor in his own tent. And when he completed his military service, he returned to his home state of South Carolina, started a family, and launched his own business in the concrete industry.

Eight kids later, Jane's dad had a thriving concrete business and a big house in the country where he shared the compound with three of his sisters and their families. He was a tough leader of his family and demanded that everyone (boys and girls alike) contribute. He was adamant that girls and boys would get the same education and

FOCUSING ON WHAT'S MOST IMPORTANT

be expected to do the same things. The kids were all required to take classes in math and science, even if they didn't like it or if they weren't gifted in these subjects. "A solid understanding of math and science is essential," he'd remind them.

"Hey, Jane. What are you still doing here?"

Startled from her daydream, Jane looked up.

"The canteen's closing in a few minutes. Better get there now if you want anything to eat," her colleague remarked.

Jane's trance was broken. She had been sitting in that post-voting room for more than an hour. It was time to get a pilot's lunch—a Coke and a Snickers bar—even if it meant facing more harassment. The battle was over. The guys had won the vote. But the war was not yet decided. Jane could and would prove them wrong.

Flight school was hard. It was demanding physically, mentally, and emotionally. The awesome responsibility of being accountable for the safe return of a multi-million-dollar aircraft never left Jane's mind. She felt personally responsible for proving that women were up to the task. And there were so many forces and unknowns in the air. It was both daunting and riveting. She thrived on the challenge.

But Jane was also struggling. Her performance in the air wasn't stellar. She was better at hitting the books, taking tests, and assimilating technical knowledge. She kept making mistakes while on test flights, and her commanders and flight instructors attributed it to her lack of confidence. In fact, one instructor told her, "You're probably the most anxious pilot I've ever flown with, and unless that changes you're out." He scheduled an "89 Ride," otherwise known as the "last chance" flight. She would have to improve significantly, or she'd be kicked out. And the rest of her team knew all about it. Some of them were already celebrating the accomplishment of Goal #5! "Women don't belong in the Air Force. Jane, you don't belong in the Air Force," they'd taunt her incessantly.

Jane was starting to believe them. Maybe she didn't have what it took to be an Air Force pilot. Maybe she was a failure. Perhaps she should drop out, like 33 percent of the others—a well-documented statistic. But her personal performance would determine whether the US Air Force would admit more females to the program. What was at stake on this flight was not only her own worth but the merit of the entire female gender. It was a heavy burden to shoulder.

It reminded her of the time she was twelve and her dad assigned her a very scary task. He decided to farm the land he owned, which meant that hundreds of tall, old pine trees had to be cleared from the property. His labor force would be his children—all eight of them. And Jane, being small, nimble, and seemingly fearless, was assigned the task of climbing the tall pine trees and advising her father which way the trees were likely to fall given the wind conditions. Jane remembers climbing those trees and being very afraid, but she had a job to do. People were counting on her. So she climbed.

This memory reminded Jane what she was made of. Being afraid wasn't going to stop her from doing her very best in the fighter pilot training program. The night before her "last ride," she pulled herself away from the crowd of boisterous male peers to have some quiet time. Centering on her faith and her supportive family, she breathed in all that her dad had taught her. If he believed in her, she could believe in herself. She had this!

The next morning, Jane woke up with a calm confidence and was focused on the task at hand. She showered, dressed, and made her way to the flight line. She felt insulated from the morning ritual of harassment by her peers. Their words and taunts fell off her like water droplets. She was determined. She knew she would ace the 89 Ride. And so she did. In fact, following the landing of her flight test, her instructor said, "That was a near-perfect flight. I've never seen you so calm and confident. You pass."

And that's how Jane broke the fifth team goal of Class 82-05. There would be a woman graduating from this Air Force flight school. There would be one woman out of sixty cadets who would earn the prestigious honor of wings in the US Air Force. The boys would have to suck it up and accept a woman as their peer. Women can fly. Women *will* fly. Women will serve honorably in the US Air Force. Jane pioneered that opportunity for herself and all women.

This is not the end of Jane's fearless Shero's Journey. She had to prove herself again and again in her career, including flying a Boeing 777 aircraft as a captain for Federal Express for twenty-nine years. She continued to get grief from male colleagues who didn't believe that women should be pilots, but it no longer bothered her. By focusing on what was most important to her, she became a fearless and fabulous pilot and the leader in charge.

Valuable Lessons Learned

Both of these stories remind us of the incredible courage, boldness, and staying power it takes to be a pioneer in a male-dominated field. There are virtually no role models. No mentors. No peer support. All that's there is our own compelling motivation—a powerful *why* that reminds us of what's most important when "the establishment" torments, taunts, and rejects us.

For Sylvia, her Shero's Journey began with incorporating the wisdom her grandmother and mother instilled in her to overcome prejudice. She then blended her feminine quality of compassion with resilience to become a leader of service and form her holistic leadership expression.

For Jane, her Shero's Journey began with developing confidence and wisdom through the teachings of her dad. And, rather than rejecting them, she embraced her female nature and innate abilities. She has since become an inspiring fearless leader. She beat the guys at their own game while maintaining her grace. Her boldness opened the skies for more women to fly to new heights in their careers.

Jane's current passion is encouraging more girls and women to become pilots. She does this in several ways, including in her role as past president of the Rotary Club of Greenville in South Carolina. Isn't it fascinating that Jane's success, as well as that of other women interested in serving their communities through Rotary Clubs, was possible only because of the fearless leadership of Sylvia Whitlock? Sylvia didn't just impact her field of education, she challenged the status quo, and in doing so she changed the world of service organizations.

What we discovered in these women wasn't just one moment of fearlessness but a lifetime of boldness, resilience, and confidence in themselves. The barriers they faced may have been cruel and unfair, but their ability to be resilient and persevere has opened the doors for other women to pursue their goals and dreams more freely.

* * * * *

In the next chapter, you'll hear from two more fearless female leaders whose stories will show you why you must start to build your success team. Going it alone will only delay and diffuse your leadership impact. Your Shero's Journey will be so much better when you learn to ask for help and enlist others in your mission.

CHAPTER 7

Developing Success Teams

Alone we can do so little. Together we can do so much.
~Helen Keller

Meet Opal Lee and Eva Hausman. Both women are global difference makers, both had teaching careers, and both are products of families who were persecuted. Yet both were able to pass on courage, hope, and determination to their children and their grandchildren. This generational strength comes from deep within them, and through that strength they achieved greater things than if they had tried to go it alone.

A key to their success was the decision to engage others in their mission and work. They collaborated and enrolled others, they undertook risky ventures, and they led fearlessly. They didn't limit their success by doing it all themselves. As a result, their positive impacts have been magnified a thousandfold. Each of us is better for having them in our world. As you read their stories, think about how you might be able to aid them and help continue their work and legacies.

Ms. Opal Lee
The Fearless Face of Freedom

If you ask Ms. Opal Lee what she does for a living, she'll reply, "I'm really just a little old lady in tennis shoes, getting in everybody's business and having a good time doing it."[48] Sounds harmless enough. But then you find out that in 2022 she was nominated for a Nobel Peace Prize.[49] And a year before that, she was invited to the White House by President Joe Biden to witness the signing of a law declaring a new federal holiday known as Juneteenth.[50] Then you discover that this wasn't the first time this "little old lady" sought an audience with the president of the United States. So you may be wondering what makes this ninety-seven-year-old lady from Texas so respected and so fearless as to command the attention of world leaders.

Known as the "Grandmother of Juneteenth," Opal Lee has spent a good portion of her life passionately advocating to have Juneteenth recognized as a major event in American history. Why, you ask? You see, it was on June 19 in the year 1865 that African American slaves in Texas finally learned of their new freedom. It had taken two-and-a-half years for the people in Texas to learn that President Abraham Lincoln had signed the Emancipation Proclamation on January 1, 1863, declaring "that all persons held as slaves" within rebellious states "are, and henceforward shall be free."[51] But not until June 19, 1865, when Major General Gordon Granger of the US Army, accompanied by US Colored

---

[48] This and all quotes from Opal Lee within this chapter are taken from the following: Opal Lee, interview with Kathy McAfee, August 24, 2021.

[49] Jay Wallis, "Members of Congress Nominate Texas' Opal Lee for Nobel Peace Prize," WFAA-TV, last modified August 18, 2023, https://www.wfaa.com/article/news/local/opal-lee-nominated-nobel-peace-prize/287-924dfd36-69ff-4b4a-84d3-4b10214883dd.

[50] Jim Saska, "Juneteenth Is Now a Federal Holiday, as Biden Signs Bill," Roll Call, June 17, 2021, https://rollcall.com/2021/06/17/juneteenth-is-now-a-federal-holiday-as-biden-signs-bill/.

[51] "The Emancipation Proclamation," National Archives, last modified January 28, 2022, https://www.archives.gov/exhibits/featured-documents/emancipation-proclamation?_ga=2.101893444.494502383.1684326284-213107575.1683210851.

Troops, arrived to the town of Galveston, did the law reach Texas. General Granger and his team nailed General Order No. 3 to the door of what's now called Reedy Chapel AME Church. It boldly stated, "The people are informed that, in accordance with a proclamation from the Executive of the United States, all slaves are free."[52]

The good news of freedom spread like wildfire. The celebrations across the state were called "Juneteenth," a combination of the words "June" and "nineteenth," and would be remembered and celebrated for years to come by millions of Americans.

But being *told* you're free and *living* free are two very different things. Opal Lee was to discover that reality in a very traumatic way. In 1939, her family purchased their first home in Fort Worth, Texas. In those days, housing was scarce and difficult to find for Black families because not all White families would sell homes to them. Even though slavery had officially ended seventy-five years earlier, American culture continued to be dominated by attitudes and actions of discrimination, segregation, and racism, effectively limiting the freedoms and opportunities for people of color.

Opal remembers her parents working extremely hard, taking multiple jobs in order to save enough money to buy their first family home. Her mother used the money she got for injuries she incurred while riding a public bus. After a great deal of searching, they finally found a small home they could afford with an owner who was willing to sell to a Black family. The neighborhood was made up mostly of White people, but the real estate agent told them everything would be just fine. No issues or concerns. So they moved in, and Opal's mom began setting up the house. "She fixed it up real nice," recalls Opal. The first few days living in the new house were joyful for twelve-year-old Opal, her two brothers, and her parents. But something terrible was about to happen.

In the early evening on the fifth night in their new home (which just happened to fall on June 19), an angry White mob gathered outside of their home. They carried guns, shovels, sticks—and their hate. The

---

[52] "War Department General Order 143: Creation of the U.S. Colored Troops (1863)," National Archives, Milestone Documents, accessed August 9, 2023, https://www.archives.gov/milestone-documents/war-department-general-order-143.

anger spread as the mob demanded that Opal and her family "get the hell out of our neighborhood." Police stood by but did nothing to control the mob. When Opal's father pulled out his rifle, the police officers promptly told him that if he so much as "busted a cap," they would sic the mob on him. As the crowd swelled to the size of five hundred people, so did the hostilities. Opal's parents made the fearless decision to send their three kids to a friend's house a few blocks away for safekeeping as they bravely stayed behind to defend their home. But the threat of violence continued to escalate, and Opal's parents fled for their lives under the cover of darkness.

The angry White mob tore Opal's house to pieces. They destroyed all the furniture, desecrated family heirlooms, and eventually burned the house to the ground. Despite the presence of police during the attack, no one was ever named, indicted, or prosecuted for the crime. There would be no justice. Opal's family never received any compensation for their losses. They endured a virtual hurricane of human hatred, and like many other Black families, all they could do was move on and begin the process of rebuilding their lives. Unfair. Cruel.

"We weren't the only Black family who suffered in this way," remembers Opal Lee. "Other Black families also had their homes threatened. Many of them defended their property with firepower. Some were successful in warding off the White vigilantes. But we were not so lucky. We lost everything that day. It's ironic really that this traumatic event happened to me and my family on June 19th. Perhaps that's why I have since been so passionate about Juneteenth. We can't take our freedom for granted."

In the days and weeks that followed, Opal and her family were supported by friends in their community. Opal doesn't remember her parents ever talking about what happened, at least not when the kids were present. What she remembers most is how doubly hard her parents worked after the incident. "They worked and worked and worked," she recalled. Having a home for the family was a huge motivation.

Opal's parents eventually saved up enough money to buy another home. As it happened, they found one a few blocks away from their last one. But that short distance was enough of a safety net for her family to coexist peacefully without the threat of violence just because of their skin color. Opal recalls, "We lived at a time when Blacks were expected to be subservient to Whites. So you took what happened to you with a grain of salt and kept on going."

Indeed, Opal and her family kept going. Resilience doesn't even begin to describe the character of this family. They were fearless and undeterred. They fully committed to building a good life and a good future for their children and their grandchildren.

Education was part of that grand plan. From the time Opal was a youngster, her mother talked to her about the importance of getting a college education. Even though Opal's mother didn't finish high school, she was adamant that education was the way out of poverty. So you can imagine how disappointed her mother was when Opal fell in love with a boy she met at high school and married him. Her mother was so mad that she didn't even attend the wedding ceremony.

Once Opal began having children—four babies in four years, to be exact—there was no time or energy left for her to go to college. She did what she had to do. And she faced difficult choices with objectivity and practicality. Soon she realized that being married to her husband was more like raising another child than having a true partner, so she moved back home with her mother. She and her four young children were welcomed back, which allowed Opal to enroll in and graduate from college. "My momma was one tough lady," Opal recalls. "She was my mentor and biggest supporter. She was determined to educate all her children, including me. She was going to see that done no matter how long it took. You see, in our community, education was the only way out."

Champion of Children's Education

With her mother's support in helping to raise her children, Opal focused on her studies. She was a diligent and eager student, thirsty to learn: "I really wanted to be a librarian, but the coursework was longer and more expensive than to become a teacher. And I was responsible for four children at home, so it only made sense to choose the quicker path." She earned her Bachelor of Arts degree in 1953 from Wiley College, a private, historically Black, liberal arts college in Marshall, Texas. She returned to Ft. Worth and taught at Amanda McCoy Elementary School for fifteen years, where she was regarded as one of the best educators of children. Third grade classrooms were her domain. As a single parent of four kids on a teacher's salary, Opal also worked a night shift at a manufacturing company to make ends meet.

But she didn't stop at just teaching inside the classroom. She also served as a "visiting teacher" (a.k.a. homeschool counselor) to provide much needed support and resources to families with children who were missing too much class time due to overwhelming circumstances. "It was my responsibility to find out and alleviate the situation," she notes. "Sometimes it was a lack of shoes and clothing. Sometimes there was no food in the house. Sometimes the electricity was cut off. And sometimes they didn't even have a place to stay." Opal's compassion and ingenuity helped these families get the support they needed so that their children could be educated and have a chance at a better life. "You know, you can't teach a child if he's hungry," she believes. Opal loved the community-based nature of her work and continued in the role as homeschool counselor for the Fort Worth Independent School District until her retirement in 1977.

Feeder of People

Opal Lee couldn't just retire. Instead, she launched herself into the new and exciting field of social impact and community activism. Among other things, Opal put her energy and influence into the preservation of Black history, the establishment of cultural landmarks and affordable housing, and the eradication of food insecurity. She also served on the board of a food bank where she and her team acquired a donation of a 33,000 square foot facility after their original location was burned to the ground by arson. It took about a year to turn it into a viable operation, but it's currently serving more than five hundred families a day. When that still didn't feed enough people, Opal started an urban farm: "I may have retired from education, but people still needed things. And they came to me for help and ideas."

Defender of History

In 2016, at the age of eighty-nine, Opal got a big idea. She decided she was going to talk some sense into Congress: "I say, you need to make yourself a committee of one. People who are not on the same page as you are, why, you can help to change their minds. It's not easy, and it won't happen overnight. But if people can be taught to hate, they can be taught to love. I believe that if each one of us would teach one of us, minds would change and we'd be in good shape."

Her positive thinking was contagious, and soon others asked what they could do. She suggested they accompany her on the long walk to the nation's capital. You see, Opal Lee planned a symbolic walk across the 1,400 miles from Texas to Washington, DC, to talk to then-President Obama about Juneteenth becoming a National Day of Observance. This was the start of the Opal's Walk 2 DC campaign, which was spearheaded by her granddaughter Dione Sims and included a massive online petition that garnered 1.5 million signatures.[53] Her efforts didn't go unnoticed, but Congress wasn't moved to act. Not yet. This little old lady from Texas wasn't deterred or dissuaded. Once she starts something, she intends to see it through.

Wielder of the Power of the Pen

Feeling the ground swell with support, Opal doubled down on her mission. She decided to express her First Amendment rights by writing a children's book for young readers. In 2019, she published a book entitled *Juneteenth: A Children's Story* because she believes that children deserve to know the truth, the real history of our nation, no matter how unpleasant. And you know how the saying goes, if we don't remember history, it's destined to repeat itself.

In early 2021, Opal received some amazing news. A bipartisan committee had introduced bill S.475, which instated the Juneteenth

---

[53] "The Real Opal Lee," Opal's Walk 2 DC, accessed August 9, 2023, https://www.opalswalk2dc.com/about#.

FEARLESS FEMALE LEADERS

National Independence Day Act.[54] It was cosponsored by sixty US senators and passed the full chamber unanimously. The House of Representatives then voted to approve the new bill. On June 17, just two days before Juneteenth, President Biden, standing alongside Vice President Kamala Harris, signed into law Juneteenth as the twelfth federal holiday.

Recognizing the heroic and persistent efforts of Opal Lee, the Biden Administration invited her to the signing ceremony held in the East Room of the White House. "Great nations don't ignore their most painful moments. They embrace them,"[55] Biden told the crowd, which included dozens of politicians, activists, and community leaders. Opal recalls, "This was a moment that I had been working towards all my life. Juneteenth as a federal holiday is an acknowledgment that Black History is American History. It still gives me goosebumps to think about."

Now, with her mission accomplished, you'd think Opal would take it easy. Instead, she celebrated her ninety-sixth birthday (October 7, 2022) surrounded by family and friends who gathered at a local diner for a watch party. This was the day that Nobel Peace Prize winners were being announced. Opal had been nominated for her lifetime work promoting peace, democracy, and civil society. While she didn't win the prize that day, she still feels like a winner having accomplished her mission with the help of so many people.

Opal Lee is a true testament to fearlessness. She, her family, and her community persevered through many hardships. They kept moving. And Opal learned to use humor to smooth over the rough patches and to connect with others. You can almost hear the laughter and joy in the background of her quotes. It's how others resonated with her message and why it was so easy for her to get 1.5 million signatures on a petition.

---

[54] "S.475 - Juneteenth National Independence Day Act," Congress.gov, last modified June 17, 2021, https://www.congress.gov/bill/117th-congress/senate-bill/475/text.

[55] Marty Johnson and Alex Gangitano, "Biden Signs Juneteenth Bill: 'Great Nations Don't Ignore Their Most Painful Moments,'" the Hill, June 17, 2021, https://thehill.com/homenews/administration/559057-biden-signs-juneteenth-bill-great-nations-dont-ignore-their-most/.

Through it all, Opal learned that teams get more things done, and faster: "You can be a committee of one, and indeed I have had success doing just that. But when you share your vision and invite people to join you on the journey towards freedom and change, then, my goodness, anything is possible!"

Eva Hausman
Fearless in the Face of Indifference

Sunday mornings were very special to Eva and her husband Irwin, especially since becoming empty nesters. No more running around taking care of everyone else's needs. This was their time. As she flipped through the special August 2009 edition of the *New York Times*, Eva became immediately transfixed. The magazine was profiling a soon-to-be-released book called *Half the Sky*, written by investigative journalists Nicholas Kristof and his wife Sheryl WuDunn. Eva was an avid reader of Kristof's *New York Times* opinion column. But that morning she learned something so shocking and riveting that it would prompt her into immediate fearless action.

"Irwin, you've got to read this article!" she exclaimed. "It's incredible what's happening. Millions of women around the world are suffering from extreme poverty and violence. And all that's needed to change this is educating girls."

Looking up from his newspaper, Irwin said nothing. Eva's interruptions had become commonplace for Sunday mornings. Ever-patient and loving, he simply replied, "Perhaps you should order the book?"

"Done!" she replied.

Eva found it difficult to settle back into her peaceful Sunday morning routine. The duality of feelings—shock and awe mixed with curiosity and unknowingness—propelled her out of the house. Blowing off her scheduled exercise class, Eva grabbed the car keys and drove straight to the Simsbury Library, where she ran into the director, Susan Bullock. Eva briefed her on what she had just read in the *New York Times* and then asked Susan if she'd help her get the word out. Susan, a fearless female leader in her own right, offered to make multiple sets of copies of the article so that Eva could send them to her friends and inform them of what she had just learned.

Upon receiving her copy of *Half the Sky*, Eva immediately tore into the pages. She couldn't put it down. It was all-consuming—life-changing, even. One particular story in the book haunted her. It was about a thirteen-year-old Ethiopian girl who was married off to an abusive man and became pregnant.[56] Realizing that she and her baby would be in danger if she stayed in the current situation, the girl ran away. She made it back to her village in time to give birth, but there was no money for a midwife. She suffered seven agonizing days of obstructed labor with the baby stuck inside her birth canal. The baby died, and this poor girl suffered serious injuries including a debilitating fistula. Her life would be plagued by ongoing incontinence, shame, and social stigma. Thinking she was cursed, the villagers refused to help her. They moved her to a hut at the edge of the village and removed the front door so that the wild animals could get to her and put her out of her misery. By nightfall the hyenas came for her. She fearlessly defended herself by waving a stick in her hand and shouting at them. She survived that night, but she knew she had to leave this perilous place or she'd die a horrible death. Once again, she had to run away to save her own life. Fortunately, she was rescued by the compassionate medical team at Addis Ababa Fistula Hospital in Ethiopia.

The mental images of this young girl fighting off the hyenas dwell in Eva's head to this day. "No mother deserves this kind of cruel indifference, no matter how poor or uneducated she is, no matter her circumstance, no matter what country she lives in or how the culture or government treats women in her country. We can and must do better," she proclaimed.

Eva learned from the book that the cost to repair a fistula was somewhere in the range of $300. She had an idea: she decided to do a fundraiser for the Fistula Foundation. She would engage her circle of influence—the forty-three people on her list to whom she had mailed the *New York Times* article—to help her raise money. These like-minded

---

[56] Nicholas D. Kristof and Sheryl WuDunn, *Half the Sky: Turning Oppression into Opportunity for Women Worldwide* (New York: Vintage Books, 2010), 93–102.

women and men became her success team. They began asking family and friends for $20 donations, and Eva even secured a $5,000 grant from a friend who worked at the Oak Foundation. At the end of two weeks, they had raised $10,000 for the Fistula Foundation. It all happened so fast. Eva was over the moon with gratitude for the encouragement and support of her friends and family.

Eva was feeling proud of herself and her accomplishments when she received some unexpected feedback from her daughter Kim, who implored her, "Mom, our work here is not done. We can and must do more."

Eva was momentarily speechless (a very rare occurrence). Reflecting on her daughter's challenging words, she recalled the impulsive feelings she felt on that Sunday morning before she jumped into action. What was the driving motivator that caused her to take such bold action? Why was this so important to her? And was there enough there to keep her going in this direction? To answer these questions, she pulled out her copy of that Sunday article and read it again.

"When I reread the *New York Times* article," Eva reflects, "I was reminded of the thesis of the book *Half the Sky*. The authors of the book believed that we could in fact eradicate poverty and violence against women just like we did in the nineteenth century when slavery ended. By doing this, terrorism and other maladies would decrease. It makes complete sense to me."

The academic in her went on to explain the two arguments made in the book:

> *The first part argues that the oppression of women in (most) developing countries is a devastating and under-recognized injustice that's the equivalent of slavery and that demands a moral and political movement as focused and principled as the campaign against slavery to bring it to an end. The second argument in the book discusses practical ways to create this movement and affect the change that is needed. I have never seen a more compelling call to action from a book in my life. And that's coming from someone who spent her life and career as a teacher and an activist.*

And that was enough for Eva to recommit and step up her efforts to make a difference for mothers around the world.

How is it that Eva could continue down this fearless path? How is it that one woman with a team loosely made up of forty-three friends could make such a big impact and do it so quickly and peacefully? To understand what drives someone like Eva Hausman, we must go back to her Leadership Origin Story.

Eva is the daughter and sister of Holocaust survivors. Her mother escaped Nazi Germany with her young son Harry and fled to the United States. Hitler and his antisemitic, White supremacist regime killed her grandparents and most of her extended family. They settled in Bridgeport, Connecticut, where there were jobs during wartime. Her mother met and married a new husband, and they gave birth to Eva. There were ten years between Eva and her older brother, but in many ways she felt like an only child.

Eva is also the daughter of entrepreneurs. Her parents were quite industrious. Living and working in Bridgeport, Eva's parents came up with the clever business called "Fashion on Wheels."[57] They offered a mobile service of ready-to-wear women's clothing and accessories brought directly to the customer. Housewives and their husbands could buy outfits in the comfort of their own homes. It was a cash business, but they offered credit terms as well. It was also a family affair. Her mom drove the truck, Eva schlepped the merchandise, and her dad managed the transactions and inventory. It was hard work and many hours, but the business grew. Eva has many memories of riding around the city after school helping her parents take orders and serve customers.

This entrepreneurial venture not only put food on the table and supported their lifestyle but roused ideas in Eva's head and compassion into her heart. She was exposed to a diverse group of people, including immigrants from all over the world. She listened to the stories customers told her, she empathized with the problems they faced, and she began to see herself as an advocate, a champion for the underdog:

---

[57] Michael J. Daly, "The Story of Harry's Remarkable Mother," CTPost, May 8, 2016, https://www.ctpost.com/news/article/The-story-of-Harry-s-remarkable-mother-7421563.php.

working class families, many of whom were immigrants. She became an excellent listener and an avid reader, a girl with a curious mind and the courage to stand up for what's right, and a fearless woman who speaks out against what's wrong. She had begun her fearless leader journey, a path that would empower her to have an amazing impact over her lifetime.

Eva chose a career in education and dedicated thirty years to being a high school social studies teacher. She married Irwin, an incredible partner and soulmate, and together they raised two fearless daughters, Kim and Lisa. Their family values included giving back, community service, and fighting for civil rights. Their volunteer leadership with the Anti-Defamation League earned them the prestigious honor of a Daniel R. Ginsberg Humanitarian Award.[58] They were unafraid to speak up and speak out against hatred, racism, and bigotry of any kind. In word and deed, the Hausman family was a role model of integrity, compassion, and justice.

And this is why Eva's daughter Kim had the gumption to stand up to her mother and challenge her. Together, the fearless mother and daughter took the next, bold step: they figured out a way to make a direct connection with Nicholas Kristof. Their method was nothing short of fearless networking. It involved writing a letter, attending an event, and standing in line to meet the speaker, who just happened to be Sheryl WuDunn. Eva discreetly handed her the letter and asked her to give it to Kristof personally. This risky move could've gone nowhere, but it resulted in big, beautiful things!

When Kristof received Eva's letter, he was moved. He gave Eva a shout-out in his weekly *New York Times* column on May 8, 2010, entitled, "Celebrate: Save a Mother."[59] It was in this column that Kristof planted another powerful seed in Eva's head. It was a simple idea—a play on grammar—but it became the catalyst for Eva and her small band of fearless friends.

---

[58] Randi Pincus, "Anti-Defamation League's 2011 Daniel R. Ginsberg Humanitarian Award Reception," Patch, October 19, 2011, https://patch.com/connecticut/greenwich/an--anti-defamation-leagues-2011-daniel-r-ginsberg-hu429bdd2e7d.

[59] Nickolas Kristof, "Celebrate: Save a Mother," *New York Times*, May 8, 2010, https://www.nytimes.com/2010/05/09/opinion/09kristof.html?searchResultPosition=1.

Eva recalls reading his column and feeling renewed energy and courage: "Mr. Kristof suggested that 'It's time to move the apostrophe so that it becomes not just Mother's Day, honoring a single mother, but Mothers' Day, an occasion to try and help mothers around the globe as well.' Little did I know at the time that Mr. Kristof's column would motivate a group of women, including me, to act again."

Inspired by Kristof's idea of relocating an apostrophe in the title of a public holiday, Eva, Kim, and two of their fearless friends launched the Mothers' Day Movement.[60] Each year they select a single charitable organization to be their beneficiary for that year's fundraising campaign.

Since its official inception in 2011, the Mothers' Day Movement has raised close to a million dollars for a variety of charities that do vital work in the areas of education, maternal health, clean water, food insecurity, and human trafficking. Eva considers Nicholas Kristof to be the father of the Mothers' Day Movement, the charity beneficiaries to be its children, and herself and her small team of fearless leaders to be the mothers of the movement. Eva and Kristof continue to stay in close touch.

"Our work is not finished," Eva says. "There are so many women and girls around the world—locally and globally—who need our understanding, compassion, and support, but mostly our action. Indeed, women do hold up half the sky." You can hear her pull for more participation, inviting us to join her success team.

Valuable Lessons Learned

Opal Lee used humor, confidence, and resonance to fully develop her Shero leadership. Eva Hausman intuitively knew she had to answer the call that the *New York Times* article had published. She, too, developed her Shero leadership first by resonating with the story and then by inspiring others to also take action.

---

[60] http://www.mothersdaymovement.org/.

DEVELOPING SUCCESS TEAMS

It is fearless leaders like Opal Lee and Eva Hausman, women who are willing to do the hard work and engage others in their vision, who will make a difference for women and girls everywhere. As Opal likes to say, "Whatever you're passionate about, you shouldn't let anything stop you from doing or accomplishing what you start out to do. You may have to take some detours, and some things will happen to you, but you must finish whatever you start. It doesn't matter how long it takes you. Freedom is worth it. It's worth a lifetime of effort."

What's simmering in your heart that could impact a large swath of humanity if only you had enough people to support your dream and vision? It takes courage to inspire others, and it requires a sacrifice to turn over a passion project to a team. All leaders understand both the joy and the pain of sharing ownership of their ideas. To do this successfully, you must learn how to balance delegation, accountability, and inspiration. And it's so worth it!

* * * * *

In the next chapter, you'll meet two more fearless female leaders who've dealt with life-threatening situations. They both made the fearless decision to trust that their gifts were wanted and needed. They consciously chose to stop waiting for other people's approval and to confidently walk into their own authentic brilliance. As a result, they found greater peace and purpose and have become beacons of hope and inspiration for others.

CHAPTER 8

Trusting That Our Gifts Are Wanted & Needed

*Everyone has talent. What is rare is the courage to follow
the talent to the dark place where it leads.*
~Erica Jong

Our next two fearless leaders are Paula Stone Williams and Kim Dechaine. Their Shero's Journeys required so much courage, transparency, and ultimately authenticity to overcome societal judgments that it left us speechless, in awe, and humbled. They both embody and model the true power of trusting our gifts, honoring our authentic selves, and remembering constantly that all of us are wanted and needed. Always.

In a world fraught with danger, we seem to seek out others who are just like us. As a way to protect ourselves, we reject anything that deviates from the narrow definition of how we look, how and what we think, and how we identify ourselves (color, creed, sexual orientation). That tendency both comes from and promotes fear. More importantly, a lack of diversity in our circle of influence limits our leadership potential. This book is about letting go of that kind of fear and instead welcoming the beauty, gift, and power of inclusivity.

These next two leaders show you what it really means to be a fearless and authentic leader—both the costs and the ultimate gifts. As you read these next stories, pay attention to whether you want to push the story away, ignore it, or pretend it isn't real. That's the limit of your ability to be inclusive. Be gentle with yourself. Just notice and continue reading. It will be well worth it.

Paula Stone Williams
The Fearless Face of Authenticity

Curling up in her favorite armchair with a glass of iced tea and a light meal, Paula Stone Williams was excited to watch the much-anticipated final episode of her favorite television series *LOST*. Paula had been a devoted fan of this series for the past six years, and now it was coming to an end.

But all good things must come to an end, and the writers of the *LOST* series certainly did it in style. When Paula realized that her favorite character, Jack, had been called by the God figure to die, she stopped breathing. She felt as if God was speaking directly to her through this show, at that very moment. With overwhelming emotion, she burst into tears, and she sobbed uncontrollably into the wee hours of the night. When she awoke in the morning, she was certain that she had heard the voice of God. She too was being called to die; to say goodbye to her life as a man, a husband, a father, and a leader so that she could transition into a woman and begin to live her authentic life.

It would take another two years until Paula would act on this calling to be authentic. Could she really go through with it? Was she brave enough? Bold enough? Was she ready to risk everything, including her family, marriage, and successful career? Who would be hurt in the process? How would this impact her three grown children? And what about Cathy, her partner with whom she had built a wonderful life for the past forty years? Was she ready to end her marriage and give up everything she had built? Was she ready to accept total rejection by all that she knew and loved?

TRUSTING THAT OUR GIFTS ARE WANTED & NEEDED

The next several years were tumultuous, filled with inner conflict, self-doubt, depression, and fear. But one thing was for certain: Paula knew she was meant to be a girl. She had recognized this truth when she was three years old. As a child, she used to dream that a "gender fairy" would come to her, wave a magic wand, and transform her body into the one she was supposed to have. But alas, no gender fairy ever showed up. Paula, who had been born into a boy's body and was given the name Paul by her parents, would have to find a way to fit in and to live her true life in secret. This challenge was further complicated by the fact that her family was deeply rooted in the evangelical church with its fundamental theology and teachings. What Paula knew, felt, and thought about her true self was considered a sin in the eyes of her church. There was only one way forward for her: she had to mask her identity, stymie her thoughts, and suppress her feelings. "I didn't hate being a boy," Paula reflects, "I just knew I wasn't one. So I just lived my life as best I could as Paul."

Life as a boy had many advantages. Paul was encouraged to be confident, smart, accomplished, and outgoing. He was groomed to be a leader early on in his life. Opportunities just presented themselves to Paul, including an offer to be a local radio host and personality. As a teenager this was a super fun, paying job that exposed him to tons of interesting and influential people. At the time, there were no girls doing this kind of work. Paul also immersed himself in singing, joined a choral group, and discovered that he had a pretty good singing voice. His vocal skills and passion blossomed into even more opportunities, including having his own band that performed and traveled to different parts of the country.

But there was a clear expectation that Paul join the ministry and build a career in church leadership. After all, that's what Paul's father had done, and his uncles too. The roadmap for Paul's career and life was laid out early on, and he obediently followed the path. He attended Kentucky Christian University and received an education in religious studies, then went on to earn a master's degree in ministry and a Doctor of Ministry in Pastoral Care. He became a pastoral counselor and a teaching pastor at two megachurches and served as CEO of a nonprofit religious organization that specialized in "church planting."

He had impressive credentials and built a strong platform, and he was highly respected by his peers and loved by his friends. By all measures, Paul was extremely accomplished in his career. Best of all, he loved preaching. And he was damn good at it too!

But Paul was still leading a double life. On the outside, he was a successful man who was greatly admired. On the inside, she was trapped in the wrong body, unable to be the person she was meant to be. She continued to carry on in the best way she could. She suffered with gender dysphoria from puberty well into adulthood. This growing unease with being in a man's body made her life ever more difficult. Other than professional therapists, there was really no one she could confide in. But there was her soulmate, Cathy, who Paul had married during college. Together they raised three children and built a solid life together.

Paul loved being a parent. Raising his son and two daughters with his wife brought him great joy and deep satisfaction. And this role continues to be the greatest source of pride and joy for Paula: "Being a parent, and now a grandparent, is what I am most proud of in my personal life."

While most parts of life were coming together at this time, Paul's gender issues were becoming more problematic. When he first entered therapy, he was still operating from a map that said gender dysphoria was "paraphilia" (a clinical term used for sexual disorders) that needed to be overcome. Working closely with skilled therapists, Paula came to understand that gender dysphoria is *not* paraphilia. In fact, gender identity, like sexual identity, is at the core of a person's being. To deny it is to deny permission to be authentic.

Despite this deep, personal work in therapy, Paula was keenly aware that she wasn't acting on the call of authenticity. The decision to transition genders was a daunting one. Paula knew it would make her life much harder and would likely inflict pain on the people she loved the most—Cathy and the kids.

To resolve the paradox, Paula reflected on the clarifying question that she often asked her clients who sought help through pastoral counseling when struggling with big decisions: "If you say yes to this, will the decision enhance your life or diminish it?" Paula first learned to ask this question from Jungian analyst James Hollis. It's a far better question than the one we commonly ask ourselves: "Will this decision make my life harder, or will it make my life easier?" Paula realized that if someone is looking to satisfy their soul, asking whether a decision will make their life harder or easier is the wrong question to ask. In a book she released after her transition, she explains, "We can either spend our lives searching for comfort, or we can spend our lives searching for meaning. Rarely will the two lead to the same conclusion."[61] And just like that she had her answer.

Paula's fearless decision to move forward with her gender transition did indeed enhance her life, but it also made it immensely more difficult. Once she began to share publicly that she was a transgender woman and intended to live her life as a woman, all hell broke loose. Within seven days, she lost her jobs (all of them), her income, her pension, her privilege, and her position of power in the evangelical world. Other than her family and a few true friends, everyone abandoned her. They banished her. They erased her from their lives and their religious community. She was dead to them. Her Shero's Journey was feeling more like a tragedy than a story of rebirth.

The pain of this rejection and betrayal was almost unbearable for Paula. If not for the love and support of Cathy and their adult children and grandchildren, if not for the kindness of a few strangers who extended a lifeline to Paula by inviting her to preach at their open and affirming church, Paula wouldn't have known how to keep going. It helped to know she wasn't alone when she was introduced to a local chapter of Parents, Families, and Friends of Lesbians and Gays (PFLAG), the nation's largest organization for LGBTQ+ people and their parents, families, and allies. Founded in 1973, PFLAG is committed to creating a world in which diversity is celebrated and all people are respected, valued, and affirmed.[62] For the first time in Paula's years on this earth, she was feeling seen, heard, loved, and valued for who she truly was. A woman. She had come home.

---

[61] Paula Stone Williams, *As a Woman: What I Learned about Power, Sex, and the Patriarchy after I Transitioned* (New York: Atria Books, 2021), 76.

[62] "About Us," PFLAG, accessed August 9, 2023, https://pflag.org/about-us/.

Rebuilding her new life took a little more time than she expected, but in the end it was well worth it. Of the many new discoveries in her new life, Paula learned that being a woman is much harder than being a man. She wished she could've brought with her more of the White male privileges that she unknowingly had in her former life as a man, such as the obvious higher end of the wage gap. It took Paula forty-eight months to earn the same amount of money she had earned in just two months when she was a man. There were also small but irritating things, such as constantly being interrupted by men and having her statements be questioned and doubted by others as if she didn't know what she was talking about.

She also discovered how tough women can be on one another. She noticed how men—especially alpha males—are respected, supported, and even empowered by other men. Alpha women, on the other hand, despite their natural leadership abilities, are frequently criticized, punished, and held back when working within hierarchical, male-dominated systems. While she thought she was "one of the good guys" in her former life as Paul, Paula in retrospect realized how much the world had been tilted in her favor when she was a man.

The unique experience of having lived life as a man and then as a woman has given Paula a new perspective and a new platform. While she's still very committed to her work as a pastoral counselor and to deepening her own spirituality, she has decided to use her platform to raise awareness of the issues facing the LGBTQ+ community and to drive change toward greater gender equality. Paula's first TEDx talk entitled "I've Lived as a Man & a Woman—Here's What I Learned" has been viewed over four million times and counting. She has since given other TED Talks, including one she copresented with her son Jonathan. Shortly after that, a literary agent approached her to write a book about her experience. In June 2021, Simon & Schuster published her memoir titled, *As A Woman: What I Learned about Power, Sex, and the Patriarchy after I Transitioned*.

Paula has embraced a more inclusive and compassionate expression of Christianity, including preaching a more open and affirming doctrine. She knows firsthand that the call toward authenticity is sacred and holy, and for the greater good. And she has dedicated the rest of her life to helping others move forward and live more courageously as their true authentic selves.

Paula's Shero's Journey began with confidence and courage. It traveled through resilience until it could morph into compassion and wisdom. As the coauthors of this book, we feel that including Paula's story is very important because barriers to leadership negatively affect not just cisgender but *all* women. And "all women" includes transgender women. In fact, transgender boys and girls, women and men, and nonbinary people continue to face extreme levels of discrimination, hatred, violence, disenfranchisement, and political and societal exclusion.

We believe there is room for all of us at the leadership table, including our transgender sisters and brothers. Leaders need to be able to work with people who promote diversity in their thoughts, ideas, experiences, and lifestyles and to welcome these differences rather than see them as threats. It's the only way for true authentic leadership to arise.

Kim Dechaine
Fearless in the Face of Depression

It was just another Saturday, a day off when she could attend to her own personal needs. At that moment, laundry was the most pressing of them all. It had been a crazy busy week of teaching kids in grades 1–3, but after spending ten years in education she was used to the grind. And she was good at it. As she stood folding the clean clothes that were still warm from the dryer, Kim suddenly burst into tears, an uncontrollable sobbing and sadness that lasted for hours.

She didn't understand where this deep emotion was coming from. She had never been a crier before. Kim grew up on a working family farm and ranch in a small town in Alberta, Canada. By age five she was riding horses, and by age seven she was skillfully helping herd the cattle on her quarter horse. She had done almost every job on that farm, including baling hay and driving tractors. In fact, there wasn't a piece of farm equipment she hadn't handled. Kim was strong; she was farm tough. So why the feebleness now? What was so overwhelming about laundry and teaching school that would cause her to lose it like this?

She gave herself the necessary motivation. "Snap out of it" she said out loud, then gave herself a quick slap in the face and roughly wiped her tears away. After a couple of forceful exhales, she was able to move to the next task on her weekend to-do list.

Kim decided to keep this moment of weakness to herself. No one needed to know about this bizarre emotional outburst. She put it behind her; stuffed it away. And that seemed to work. Until the insomnia kicked in. She wrote off the first restless night as work pressure from grading assignments, planning for individual student's needs, and preparing lessons. But when she couldn't sleep the second night, or the third, she began to worry. She started feeling unusually irritable at the simplest things, she couldn't focus or remember details, and she was making careless mistakes at work. This wasn't at all like her normal in-control self. She became very anxious at night, worried about whether she'd be able to fall asleep. She decided to call in sick to work, then slept the whole day.

But the insomnia cycle continued: three nights of fitful or no sleep followed by one stay-at-home sick day. Kim's near-perfect attendance record as a teacher was now shot to hell. Afraid to ask for help, she soldiered on, telling no one of her sleep issues. She thought about asking her school principal for stress leave but couldn't bring herself to do it. People who went on stress leave were thought to be people with mental illness, that there was something wrong with them. She didn't want the stigma of mental illness following her around for the rest of her teaching career, so she quit her job after completing the school year and planned to get her act together over the summer.

But things went from bad to worse. In July she was rushed to the hospital after she suddenly and inexplicably lost her eyesight. Thinking she might have a brain tumor, doctors ran a battery of tests. Kim was in the hospital for two weeks and was getting progressively weaker. She thought she was dying, and so did her mother, who was by her side night and day. Kim was more anxious than she had ever been in her life. *Is this it? Is this how I'm going to die?* she thought.

Then she caught a break. The doctors began to experiment with various medications, and Kim started to respond positively. Within a few days, she was released from the hospital and was allowed to

TRUSTING THAT OUR GIFTS ARE WANTED & NEEDED

convalesce at home with her parents. Her strength returned, she was sleeping through the night, and her spirits were lifted. Hope was in the air.

That's when she met Brad, the love of her life. They were engaged and married within the year. Soon after that, Kim became pregnant and had a beautiful baby girl. She named her Aletta, which was the middle name of her beloved grandmother, one of the central figures in Kim's life. And then a second baby arrived, another daughter, Skylar. Kim never felt so blessed. But shortly after Skylar's birth, postpartum depression set in. This time, the darkness stayed with Kim for ten long years.

The depression got so bad that Kim would just sleep all day long. She got to the point where she couldn't get out of bed. She would muster the necessary energy to get up just to feed her two young girls, but once they were fed, Kim would crawl back under the covers, only to rise shortly before her husband would get home from work in the evenings.

She managed to go through the motions of being a mother and a wife, but deep inside she was beginning to have suicidal thoughts. There was one moment when her family went on a camping trip. Brad was pulling the kids in a Radio Flyer red wagon while Kim was walking behind them slowly. In what she describes as an out-of-body experience, Kim could see them from above and had the clarity of thought that they would be okay without her. They would go on and enjoy happy, productive lives even without a mother or a wife. This sad thought gave her an unexpected sense of peace, knowing that she could leave them and they'd be just fine.

Fortunately, Kim's journey didn't end that day. In fact, she credits her local public library with saving her life. They hired her as Director of Programs, a role that allowed her to use many of her teaching skills and engage with a variety of people outside her home. She felt useful and connected in this new environment. She could feel the spirit of the independent woman she had been before she became a mother. So she made a fearless decision to live, not die.

She soon opened up to her husband and a few trusted friends (her support team) about what she had been going through internally during these past ten painful years. She realized that she had to make herself and her well-being a priority. With that decision made, and with the love and support of those around her, Kim set out on a quest to heal herself. She met with psychologists and psychiatrists, doctors of naturopathy, and energy healers. She dug into research, read books, and attended programs to learn more about energy healing and mental health.

Within a year, Kim began to pull out of the dark hole caused by her long-term depression. She began to feel good. Really good. She realized that other people can't make us happy; we must make our own happiness. She learned that depression and mental illness are very common and that the more we talk about it, the more open and transparent we are about it, the more we can heal ourselves and others. Kim was walking in the light now, feeling alive for the first time in a very long period.

When Aletta started to experience anxiety at the age of seven, Kim's knowledge and firsthand experience helped her quickly recognize it. Kim knew it wasn't just some adolescent phase or moody girl thing. It was something to take seriously. This was something that needed immediate attention and love. Lots of love. It was during this crisis with her daughter that the big shift happened for Kim. There's no better way to explain it than the way Kim does:

> *I heard a voice. It was clear as a bell. I could feel and sense the voice. It told me that the current situation with my daughter was the exact reason why I went through my own depression: so that I could help her through her journey. Because of what I had been through myself, I had gained the compassion, the empathy, the understanding, the insight, and the ability to be a healer. I could not only help my own daughter, but I could help others, many others, heal from depression and other issues. This was my calling, and I was prepared now to answer it.*

Kim's gifts were indeed needed and wanted by many people. Kim went on to not only support and help her daughter heal from anxiety but make the fearless decision to change careers. After many years of teaching and a stint in financial planning, she stepped into entrepreneurship and confidently opened her own healing business. It has since evolved into a coaching, speaking, and educating practice for addressing issues of overwhelm and burnout. Serving as a feminine leadership coach, Kim works with women all over the world who are struggling to balance family and career—women who are feeling overwhelmed and are at risk of burnout. Knowing firsthand the high cost and consequences that working women face trying to do it all and never having enough time, Kim brings her knowledge, healing skills, and compassion to help other women reconnect with their energies and values so that they can unleash their true potential.

Today Kim is authentically leading her life, her family, and her business with gratitude and gusto. She's guided by her highest core value, which is peace, and she filters her decisions based on whether her actions and choices will result in her feeling calm and at ease. She has learned to listen to and trust her own intuition. "It's taken a lot of work, but it's worth it," she says. Her secret formula? She gives herself ample quiet time, or "slow time" as she calls it, so that she can hear and feel the truth and tap into her inner feminine power.

Speaking her truth, Kim wants us to know that "We live in a society where feminine energy is not glorified but rather suppressed, and that demands we use more masculine energy within us to operate, to belong, and to be accepted. And when we demand more masculine energy from ourselves, we get overwhelmed, burn out, have pain, or get sick." Kim wants us to see feminine energy as the "being" energy, in contrast to the masculine "doing" energy. "And when you are in your feminine energy," she says, "you are not busy doing, but instead enjoying that which is before you, being in the present moment."

Kim has a very clear point of view about what's needed in our leaders: compassion—number three of the eight great attributes of fearless leadership. She believes that "Compassion allows you to look at people through your heart and not just your head. Compassion is also essential for how you look at and connect with yourself."

Kim is a great example of the triumph and transformation that can happen when we trust that our gifts are wanted and needed. No matter what you're going through, no matter how dark and difficult, remember that the world needs what you uniquely have to offer. The world needs your gifts.

Valuable Lessons Learned

Paula's and Kim's Shero's Journeys needed an immense amount of courage, compassion, and faith. Their deeply held values boosted their resilience and allowed them to transform with authenticity and personal sovereignty. Both women, especially Paula, show us how important it is to embrace inclusivity. Without it, we're condemned to living a life of fear.

Every person born deserves to share their gifts regardless of how they come into the world. We can and must reinvent the storyline for all women. When we do, acceptance and abundance will gloriously triumph over fear and lack.

* * * * *

In the next chapter, you'll meet our final set of fearless female leaders. You'll discover how they navigated their Shero's Journeys by taking the road less traveled. Their stories remind us that we don't have to sacrifice our dreams to fit a mold or fulfill someone else's expectations. We can create our own paths and find new ways to lead.

CHAPTER 9
Creating New Ways to Lead

It was we, the people; not we, the white male citizens; nor yet we, the male citizens; but we, the whole people, who formed the Union.
~Susan B. Anthony

We'd like to introduce you to two more remarkable fearless leaders: Jolly Lux and Wendy Fong. Both women elected to break with traditional career paths and follow their dreams, even when it came at the expense of disappointing others and taking on more risks. Both took strength from their immigrant heritages and were guided by their intuition, as well as by mentors and role models in their lives. Now they serve as paragons of entrepreneurial leadership for other girls and women. There's also learning gold to be mined in Jolly's and Wendy's stories if you're a parent or grandparent of a girl or young woman. You, too, can serve as a mentor or role model. After all, it takes a village to raise a fearless female leader.

Jolly Lux
The Fearless Face of Resilience

She gathered her things as quickly and quietly as she could. She didn't have much time to make her escape, so she tossed her meager possessions into a duffle bag and headed down the stairs. She was frightened but knew deep down in her heart that better things awaited her if she could just get there.

She had no choice but to leave. She had to get out of this situation before it got any worse. What started out as a generous short-term housing offer from "friends of the family" was turning into a bizarre form of imprisonment. During the three months that she lived with this family, the mother of the household stole her money, locked her in the bedroom, and threatened to report her "unruly behavior" to her relatives if she got out of line. Surely this was not the American hospitality she had heard so much about.

As she bravely stepped out onto the street at 2:00 a.m. on a chilly November morning, Jolly felt the cold, damp breeze chill her bones. She wished she had a winter coat or a pair of gloves to keep herself warm and dry, but alas, she had none of these protective garments. Never had she experienced weather conditions like they had in Seattle, Washington. She had grown up in Uganda, a landlocked country located in East Africa, where the coldest month of the year, April, had an average temperature of about 72°F.

With thoughts of freedom warming her spirit, Jolly made her way to the bus station. She presented her ticket and climbed on board a three-day, three-night cross-country journey from Seattle to Connecticut, where she had arranged for a paid job as a live-in caretaker for an elderly couple.

The bus ride was very difficult for her. She felt chilled and feverish all over. *Perhaps the heater on the bus isn't working properly*, she thought. And then the coughing started. She did her best to suppress it so as not to disturb the other travelers, but she knew she had caught a cold, or something worse. She would deal with it when she arrived in Connecticut. For now, she just needed to hang in there. She slept as much as she could.

As she faded in and out of a sweaty state of dreamland, Jolly experienced flashbacks from her childhood in Uganda. There were many happy memories to revisit. A community of strong women had raised her, including her mother, her maternal grandmother, and four aunts. Some of the latter were just slightly older than Jolly and could've passed as her peers or sisters. All the women in Jolly's family were pious, hardworking, and believed in the power of education. They shared with Jolly what they were learning in school, and as a result Jolly learned at an early age to speak and write English, do basic math, and problem-solve long before she ever stepped foot in an official school room. These formidable women were committed to providing Jolly with a solid foundation early on. They imbued her with strong self-esteem, a love of learning, deep faith, and an innate sense of leadership.

When Jolly was six years old, her family took her to the local school to enroll her in kindergarten. The evaluators quickly realized how bright she was and recommended that she skip kindergarten and move straight into primary school. Enrolled as a day student in the all-girls Catholic school that was affiliated with her family's local parish, Jolly advanced her studies, learned how to be a good person, and discovered how to help others. She also figured out how to exercise her leadership skills in surprising and productive ways.

In middle school, Jolly stood up to "management" and negotiated a deal. She and a few of her classmates had been asked by the headmaster to go to the village well to fetch water, a necessity for the school and a normal duty regularly tasked to students. Along the way, Jolly and her classmates came upon some young kids kicking a soccer ball in an open field. They joined in the fun, even though they knew that this side-tracked activity would be frowned upon. Weighing the risks and rewards, Jolly elected to play for a while and convinced the other girls it was okay. They'd have plenty of time to fetch the water and return to school on schedule.

But when they got to the village well, there was a long line of people, much longer than normal. Jolly knew at that moment that she and the girls would be late getting back and that there would be hell to pay. She and the other girls dutifully waited in line, respecting their elders. When it was their turn, they collected as much well water as they could physically carry.

While heading back to school, Jolly started a conversation with the other girls about the severe punishment that would be waiting for them when they returned late. Most likely they'd be beaten with a cane in front of the other students. Pain and humiliation seemed an unjust punishment for the crime of being late.

"We should *not* be beaten," Jolly pronounced to the other girls as they trudged along with the heavy loads of water buckets balancing on their shoulders. "It wasn't our fault that the line was so long. There was nothing we could do about that. We had no control over this."

The more Jolly spoke, the more hope the other girls felt. "We must stand up for ourselves," they agreed. "We must reason with them."

When the girls got back to school, the headmistress was indeed angry. They were late and would be beaten as a result. Without raising her voice, Jolly stepped forward, calmly and confidently making her argument as the other girls timidly stood behind her. She explained that while a punishment for being late was in order, a beating was an excessive and unwarranted consequence for this specific situation. The headmistress listened to Jolly with respect and saw the reasoning in her argument. She decided not to beat them, but to give them a lighter sentence: extra duties in the vegetable garden.

Jolly and the girls happily accepted this sentence and "did their time" with joy in their hearts. From that point on, Jolly gained not only respect from the headmistress but a loyal following from the other students. They recognized Jolly's leadership skills. She had their backs. She was unafraid to stand up for what was right and just.

A few weeks after that experience, young Jolly was walking back home from school. It was 2:00 p.m. and the sun was high in the sky, shining hot and bright upon her. She looked up at the sun and a thought came to her: *When I grow up, I'm going to do big things in my life.* She knew at a young age that greatness was in store for her. This premonition and deep sense of purpose and possibility is what she would need to call upon as she made her way across the United States to begin her new life in Connecticut.

On the afternoon of the third day of Jolly's travels, the bus pulled into the terminal at Hartford Union Station in Connecticut. Sweaty and a bit delirious, Jolly exited the bus and immediately went to a local health clinic to get checked out by a doctor. She was shocked to be diagnosed with tuberculosis, a potentially serious infectious disease that affects the lungs. The doctors immediately assumed that she had brought the disease with her from Africa. Not knowing how contagious she was, they quarantined her in a medical ward to observe her and treat the bacterial infection.

Jolly spent the next five months in Middlesex Hospital in Middletown. In a room by herself, with only a sliver of a view of the Connecticut River to engage her imagination, Jolly once again felt alone. She was a thirty-year-old college graduate with hopes and dreams of doing amazing things, but her first six months in America had proved to be surprisingly difficult. Still, she held out hope that these initial setbacks were really blessings in disguise. She knew she had to remain strong and hopeful.

She occupied her time in the hospital the best way she knew how: she prayed, read books, and slept a lot. Her only visitors were nurses, aides, doctors, and other medical professionals, all of them masked and protected from head to foot as they came in and out of her room to take her vitals. They weren't particularly nice or kind to Jolly as they went about their business. Perhaps it was the infectious nature of the diagnosis, or maybe it was Jolly's ethnicity, but people didn't seem to want to get to know her. Most just treated her and moved on. She was grateful for their care and expertise, but she longed for conversation and friendship.

There was one helpful nurse, who suggested to Jolly that she try to do some exercises in her room to regain some strength, demonstrating a few stretches and movements. Jolly took hold of this idea and used the time and space in her hospital room to rebuild her strength. She could feel her body, mind, and spirit start to recover. After a few weeks, Jolly's tests came back as "all clear," and the doctors felt confident that she was no longer contagious. She could be safely released to the community, so they gave her clearance to work for the elderly couple who had wanted to hire her for in-home caregiving.

Once Jolly moved into the couple's house in Meriden, she began helping the couple with their daily living activities, which included preparing meals, bathing them, dressing them, and driving them to appointments. At first the adult children of the elderly couple were reluctant to have Jolly in their parents' home, but after a few visits, they realized how trustworthy, decent, caring, and loving Jolly was. She soon became like a member of their family.

Life was finally becoming brighter for Jolly. She felt at home in America and found people who respected her and treated her well. She was earning a good living and contributing by helping people, and she was making new connections in the community. She felt like she belonged. But when one of her elderly clients passed away and the family had to make other arrangements for the surviving spouse, Jolly lost her full-time job.

Because she still had time left on her immigration visa, Jolly wanted to make the most of her remaining time. So she devised a plan to go back to school and get a new degree in nursing or another helping profession. Her first college diploma in Uganda had been in the accounting field, but that didn't excite her. It was the helping professions that were a natural fit for Jolly. She had many friends who had done well as registered nurses, but Jolly had never been too keen on all the blood, fluids, and needles that nurses had to deal with. But when she heard an advertisement on the radio for a diploma in massage therapy, she thought it sounded like a wonderful career path for her. She applied and was accepted to the school.

Jolly's remarkable story doesn't end there. With her infectious spirit and a desire to give back, she ventured into the world of therapeutic massage therapy. Over the course of sixteen years, she leveraged her unique life experiences and skills to offer her clients compassionate care. Her success as a massage therapist brought her personal and financial fulfillment, allowing her to help countless individuals manage their pain and improve their well-being. She also bought a house, got married, became a Rotarian, and served on club committees for many years. A believer in paying it forward, Jolly also launched a nonprofit organization in 2011 called Guiding Light Orphans, Inc. (affectionately known as GLO), which provides medical camps, health clinics, epilepsy intervention, women's empowerment programs, and access to clean water for rural Ugandan communities.

As a result of the COVID-19 pandemic, Jolly made the difficult decision to pivot yet again. She closed her therapeutic massage business and found the courage and energy to open a brand-new business in digital and social media marketing called JAL Visionary Solutions, LLC. She continues to serve as executive director of GLO, raising funds, organizing mission trips to rural Uganda, engaging their board of directors, and motivating as many volunteers as she can. Jolly has set a goal to speak at the United Nations and to dedicate her energy to empowering women and girls to fearlessly believe in the power of their dreams and potential.

Jolly's transformation from a struggling immigrant to a thriving, dedicated, naturalized US citizen serves as a testament to her unwavering determination and resilience. This is what Jolly says to others when they are facing tough times or difficult decisions: "Don't dwell on the challenges. Rather, look for the blessings in the challenge. What is it teaching you? What are you going to do about it? How can you feel the pain of the challenge and turn it into something positive? That's what I strive to do: to feel the pain and turn it into a blessing. I like to say, 'Thank you, Challenge, you have made my life more blessed.'"

Wendy Fong
Fearless in the Face of the Old Boys' Club

Something wasn't right. The fire marshal had just left after checking the venue and validating that the facility would safely hold the crowd size Wendy and her team had planned for. She was pretty sure her competitor had called the authorities and raised a false flag designed to squelch the success of her first rave (an all-night music festival). While the inspection did delay her event opening for an hour or so, the show would go on. Enthusiastic patrons were patiently waiting for the doors to open. The chatter of two thousand fans was energizing. This was going to be a wonderful launch for Wendy's new business, Shapeshifter Productions.

Once the doors opened, people started to pour in, showing their wristbands as proof of payment. But Wendy noticed something odd. The money in the cash box for the same-day sales was very low compared to the number of people coming through the doors. She knew she didn't have many pre-event sales, so she wondered where all the money was. She asked around, casually inquiring with guests where they had purchased their wristbands. The consistent answer was that they had paid cash to the security guards in the parking lot. Wendy suddenly realized what was happening. The security team who worked for the venue were scalping the wristbands and pocketing the cash. She needed to intervene fast if she was going to save the profitability of her first event.

Boldly making her way to the dark and poorly lit parking lot, Wendy spotted two security guards. Her heart was pounding, but she found the grit to approach them. Standing at 5'6" and weighing in at a slim 120 pounds, fearless Wendy entered their personal space and demanded to know what was going on. These men looked down at her and denied any wrongdoing. She snatched the remaining wristbands from their hands and confidently announced that she was changing the process. As she made her way toward the entrance door, she couldn't believe what she had just done.

With the new procedure in place, ticket sales continued, and the cash box reflected the big success that Wendy had envisioned for that special evening. Later that night, the venue owner stopped by to check in with her to see how things were going. When she complained to him that his security guards had taken advantage of the situation, he shrugged his shoulders and blatantly told her, "Not my problem. Next time hire your own security team."

After a very long and successful night, Wendy made her way back to her apartment. She wondered what on earth she was thinking walking out into a dark parking lot all by herself and confronting two men almost twice her size. What if it had gotten physical or worse? There were not many witnesses around, and while she had trained for four years in Kung Fu during high school (and even competed in the sport), it probably wouldn't have been enough to save her life if things had gotten out of hand. How could she have been so bold? Where did her confidence come from?

Plopping herself down on the sofa, she noticed a framed picture on the bookshelf. It was a drawing she had made as a child of her and her beloved *Pau Pau* (which means "grandmother" in Cantonese). She had drawn it on the day that she, her sister, and her grandmother first arrived in America. She was only eight years old at the time, and none of them spoke English. Wendy still marvels at the courage and guts her grandmother modeled for her and her sister. She was and always will be a mentor and inspiration to her.

Pau Pau was widowed as a young woman after her fisherman husband was lost at sea after a big storm. She went on to remarry another man with whom she had several children, including Wendy's mother. They grew up in Hong Kong under British rule and survived very difficult times during the Japanese occupation of Hong Kong during World War II. No doubt these experiences made *Pau Pau* a strong and resilient woman. She was also an independent thinker and a very savvy businesswoman, especially in Hong Kong. By her mid-sixties, she started her own business that grew into what Wendy often referred to as a "tiny empire." She owned and managed a fleet of taxis and buses, as well as a mini store. All this while caring for her two granddaughters until Wendy's mother could relocate to America to marry the man who would become their father and provider.

Grabbing a family photo album from the bookshelf, Wendy started flipping through pictures of her childhood. Underneath one of the photos was a note she had written years ago that captured one of *Pau Pau's* favorite sayings: "Never forget where you come from." Wendy smiled thinking of how many stories her grandmother had told her that ended with this familiar motto.

Continuing to flip through the images and memorabilia in the family album, Wendy came upon her college graduation photo. She was the first in her family to not only graduate from college but earn a master's degree in business, a major she chose because she wanted to become an entrepreneur like her grandmother. After graduating, Wendy was recruited by Anderson Consulting. At first she accepted their generous offer to start as an analyst, but she soon got cold feet and rescinded her acceptance before the start date. What she really wanted to do was follow her bliss and expand a magazine she had started in college.

As the copublisher of *Silk Magazine*, Wendy and her college partner developed specialized editorial pieces and targeted advertising focused on serving the needs and interests of Asian Americans from Generation X. They wrote serious articles such as "Busting the Myth of the Model Minority" and "The Crisis of Southeast Asian Refugees." It was deeply satisfying work, but there were concerns about the financial side of the business. Wendy and her partner had self-funded the magazine venture using their own credit cards. Though they worked hard to find an investor and pitched to many individuals and groups, they never landed a serious investor who believed enough in their vision and mission to risk their own capital. In addition to her student loans, Wendy was creating significant debt.

To keep the magazine afloat for a few years, she quickly learned about debt refinancing and how to leverage and manage debt. The magazine soon morphed into a business with a different focus: event production and management. And that business proved to be not only profitable but sustainable. With her keen oversight, Wendy managed all financial aspects of this new business. She managed to pay off the magazine debt within two years and build up a large following of enthusiastic repeat customers who helped her build a robust brand and revenue stream. At the age of twenty-six, she then sold her interest in the business to her partner and moved to Houston to start a new career in the healthcare industry.

Wendy loved her new job but was surprised how few women held leadership positions in the company; most were at the staff level. The confidence and boldness that Wendy had cultivated running her own event production company helped prepare her to deal with the brilliant and often difficult-to-deal-with physicians, including neurosurgeons and dermatologists. She quickly realized that if she didn't stand up for herself with confidence, "People will treat me any way they wish."

Fast forward fifteen years. Wendy was hired to serve as an executive at a privately owned employee benefits company. During the interview with the regional president, Wendy remembers him telling her, "I hired you to change things around here in both diversity and operations." He went on to tell her that he needed her to be completely honest and transparent with him about whether the company stood any chance of fulfilling its strategic goals. He promised her the authority to make necessary personnel changes *at every level*. Last, he clarified that his organization believed in and practiced meritocracy and that "No one is off the table," meaning that anyone could be fired for not upholding company values, even those at the highest level of leadership.

CREATING NEW WAYS TO LEAD

Wendy recalls that during one of her first executive meetings, she looked around and noticed she was the only woman in the room, and the only minority. "At that moment, I realized that my presence allowed them to check off two boxes for this division: 1) woman on the leadership team, and 2) minority on the leadership team. Mission accomplished!" Wendy soon discovered that *wanting diversity* and *being inclusive* are two very different things. Culturally shifting this company was going to take some doing.

While leadership hired her to change the organization's "male, pale, and stale" perception, and though diversity was reinforced by discussion, reality was very different. Wendy began to feel like she was opening one Pandora's Box after another, discovering increasingly more issues that needed to be addressed. With the amount of resistance she faced, Wendy knew the Old Boys' Club was alive and well in her organization.

The next thing she encountered was microaggression. One particularly ironic example came in the form of being left off a calendar invitation for an important DEI (now DEIB) leadership meeting. Being the only person of color at that level, it was clearly a place where Wendy's voice and expertise would be of high value. Was this oversight an accident? She reached out to Steve, the Caucasian male leader who was spearheading the DEI initiative. Based on the obvious discomfort during the call, Wendy figured out that he had indeed deliberately left her off the list. She was effectively uninvited to the table. She chalked this up to the fact that she wasn't "the docile model minority that many Asians have the reputation of being or is expected of them."

Nevertheless, Wendy was soon given an important project analyzing a research study called "The Voice of the Customer." One of the findings was linked to the underperformance of a key leader in the company who happened to be a family member and a close ally to the regional president. Yes, nepotism had been part of the company's hiring practices since its inception. No one had bothered to challenge this policy over the years that the company had grown and expanded into a more professional organization. The issue clearly needed to be discussed in this meeting. Knowing she was already on thin ice with her boss, Wendy summoned as much intellectual courage as she could to speak truth to power and to do right by the company. Shortly thereafter, she was fired from her job.

Does Wendy regret having made the fearless decision to tell the truth and speak her mind? Absolutely not. She realizes that this firing had absolutely nothing to do with the quality of her work, her integrity, or her job performance. She was fired because she had rocked the boat. She was fired because they didn't want her in "the club." This seemed like a clear case of wrongful dismissal.

Evaluating her options to challenge the company in court, Wendy sought the advice of attorneys at the Equal Employment Opportunity Council, who told her it was a solid case. Her friends, who had either witnessed or been through similar issues, told Wendy that it would be a very long, emotionally draining, and difficult battle. In the end, Wendy decided it wasn't worth the extra fight.

When confronted with the difficult choice between remaining silent and compliant to keep your job and fit in or being brave and speaking your mind at the risk of being fired, Wendy advises, "There's only one good choice: to do the right thing. Always."

Wendy turned this difficult experience into her signature story for her new consulting business, Chief Gigs,[63] where she strives to prevent events like this from happening to others. People respond very positively whenever she shares her story. But Wendy's real victory—one inspired by her grandmother—was to become an entrepreneur and build her own tiny empire.

Valuable Lessons Learned

Jolly and Wendy listened to their intuition. They trusted that they would make the right choices in some difficult situations. As all of ours do, their Shero's Journeys began with integrating their masculine and feminine qualities of leadership. They required the confidence and internal fortitude to succeed no matter what. These two fearless leaders needed to find resilience in following their dreams. To fulfill their

---

[63] https://chiefgigs.com/.

destinies, they needed focus and clarity to become wise and bold. As a result, their journeys took exciting turns that allowed them to discover and create new ways to lead.

If you, dear reader, find yourself in a moment of doubt or confusion, please find a mentor or trusted confidant who can hold your vision until you can pick it up yourself.

* * * * *

In our final chapter, we outline the actions you can take to make the individual, societal, and structural changes necessary to pave the way for more women to ascend and succeed in leadership and positions of influence:

- We challenge you to take specific action to help you and those you care about become more fearless leaders.
- We invite you to pay it forward by actively helping other women and girls overcome barriers to leadership.
- We empower you and your organizations to invest more time, energy, and resources into fearless female leadership.

In this way, we can and will rewrite the narrative of the Shero's Journey, ensuring that women and girls can succeed and realize their full leadership potential. And when that happens, everyone wins!

CHAPTER 10

Changing Everything

There's a moment when you have to choose whether to be silent or stand up.
~Malala Yousafzai

The 2023 Nobel Memorial Prize in Economic Sciences was awarded to Claudia Goldin for advancing our understanding of women's labor market outcomes. Her seminal work has validated that over the last several hundred years the barriers to equal pay and opportunities have become harder to overcome for married women and women with children. According to the Royal Swedish Academy, "Society has experienced significant political, social, and technological changes. Contemporary industrialized countries have enjoyed steady economic growth since the Industrial Revolution. It would be easy to believe that women's participation in the labor force would follow the same trend, but Goldin's research has shown that this is not the case."[64]

It's time for all of us to step up and stop overlooking and undervaluing women's leadership contributions and potential.

Our goal in writing this book is to make room for *everyone* at the leadership table, including you, whether you're leading a corporation,

---

[64] "The Sveriges Riksbank Prize in Economic Sciences in Memory of Alfred Nobel 2023," NobelPrize.org., accessed November 30, 2023, https://www.nobelprize.org/prizes/economic-sciences/2023/popular-information/.

a small business, a family, or your own life. Over the past several years, we've seen women losing ground in each of these areas at an alarmingly rapid rate. We must turn that around. And that means we need change at both the individual and societal levels, including a structural overhaul, now.

While this book is about female leadership, the point is that when women are heard and recognized as leaders, they open the doors for everyone. That's why we've defined a new Shero's Journey to incorporate masculine *and* feminine leadership behaviors, traits, and methodologies so that whole leaders can emerge. Ultimately, we want to create a system that allows people to incorporate all of themselves into their leadership descriptions.

Most men get the concept that being a leader doesn't require perfection. In fact, they understand that being a leader is messy work. They know that if you're not getting dirty, if you're not struggling, if you're not dealing with your fears, you're not truly doing the work of fearless leadership.

While women inherently understand this, we somehow seem to think it doesn't apply at work. If you've ever raised a child or were actively involved in a child's life, you know what we're talking about. Kids are messy, and running a household is demanding, yet many women feel that unless they're *invited* to the leadership table at work, they're not leaders. They think they need permission to lead at work. Or worse, they think they need to be liked to lead at work. We shared some stories of incredible women who changed their circumstances and impacted the next generation of women to remind you that it's in *you* to do that too. There's a fearless leader within you. Take your own Shero's Journey to find and empower your leadership.

You may be wondering how to go about that or where to start. Consider that you may find yourself in one of three places:

1. You clearly see actions to take in any of these three categories: a) Yourself; b) Society; c) Alignment of systems and structures.
2. You know that changes are needed but don't know where or how to start.
3. You think it's hopeless, that too much needs to change, and there isn't enough time to get it all done.

Ultimately, you might think that only someone else who's stronger, better, and smarter than you can tackle challenges like these, so it's probably best to just suck it up and accept the inevitable: the ever-declining status for women; defeat; game over; hello housework. We say hell no. Hell no to surrendering our professional potential for a life of domestic servitude.

Channeling Your Inner Fearless Leader

The world needs you. Now. Just as you are. We know you're the one and that as an individual you *can* affect change. You can take any one of the steps we suggested in this book and apply it. Even making one small change is enough to change the system:

- If you haven't already done so, discover your personal brand or write your Leadership Origin Story.
- Create your Fearless Leader Manifesto that visually expresses who you are right now as a fearless leader.
- Each month, take on one of the eight great attributes of fearless leadership and find ways to express that characteristic.
- Get into a book club and talk about this book. Check out the study guide provided in the back of this book.
- Pass this book along to someone you think could be a fearless female leader. Or better yet, buy a few copies of this book and gift it to your women friends. And don't forget to share this book with your manager, your team, and even the CEO of your organization. By doing so, you're embracing the wisdom of President Harry S. Truman who said, "Not all readers become leaders, but all leaders must be readers."[65]
- Be better informed as an individual. Read more articles and books, including books that are banned. Can you believe that in this day and age, and in the United States, people are actually banning books like the Nazi's did in World War II? Don't allow history to be rewritten and whitewashed. Question opinions. Look for facts. Go behind the headlines and read deeper

and broader. Study all sides of an issue. Challenge stereotypes and misinformation with your intellectual and moral courage. Become an expert.
- Start being a role model for fearless female leadership. Make a commitment to yourself to mentor others and to pay it forward. If you're in a position of influence, we encourage you to actively invest in women in your organization or network by sponsoring them into The Fearless Leader program. Visit the More Fearless Resources section at the back of this book for more details.

In these ways, you create a community of fearless leaders around you. You don't have to go it alone; you can build a support team just for you. Enrolling in The Fearless Leader eight-week group mentoring program will help you further expand your network and self-awareness. Because it's a structured environment, you can develop yourself and your leadership skills in a safe and supportive place. You can begin your Shero's Journey now by scanning the QR code at the end of this book or by visiting the website TheFearlessLeader.com.

All of this is within your power when you make the decision to become a fearless leader.

Fearlessly Changing Society

As an individual you can influence others in so many ways:

- Find ways to share your wisdom. Become a mentor to women and girls in your life and at work. Help other females advance in your workplace by building them up rather than tearing them down.
- Become an advocate and ally for women, including women of color, trans women, queer women, immigrant women, and other women who are routinely discriminated against. Find groups you can join (or create) that support changing the conversation. Stand up and speak out against racism and discrimination of all types.

- Change your media diet. Stop watching films and shows that depict women in old, stereotyped roles or include violence against women. Talk to young girls about why this is not okay. This type of entertainment media is dangerous and perpetuates an unacceptable view of women. Follow the work Geena Davis is doing to promote women in Hollywood.[65] Did you know that in the 1920s and 1930s women were the primary writers and directors? It was only when the industry shifted to film with sound that media companies, needing financing, were required to hire male writers and directors. Why? Because the financial institutions would back only men.

- Vote. Vote. Vote. Every election, small or large, is an opportunity to change the leadership dynamic for the better. Protect voting rights by getting involved in voter registration and Election Day processes. Coauthor Kathy has served as an election poll worker, as did her grandmother Rosario Garcia Davila. "It's an eye-opening experience that deepened my appreciation for our democratic institutions and the need to defend voting rights," shares Kathy.

- Make women's leadership part of the conversation and strategy at your workplace and in your community. Secure funding for women's leadership development programs in your organization (you can check your state for grants). That's free money to your company. How can they say no to free money to train women?

---

[65] "About Us," Geena Davis Institute on Gender in Media, accessed September 15, 2023, https://seejane.org/about-us.

Fearlessly Changing Workplace Infrastructure

Once you harness your power to change individually, start applying that power to others:

- Ensure you have a strong executive sponsor or sponsors and an adequate budget to make a significant impact in the lives and careers of your female colleagues.
- Close the wage gap by demanding transparency about salaries and bonuses in the workplace.
- If you're asking for a raise or interviewing for a new job, absolutely negotiate the compensation package (not just the base salary). Research conducted by authors Linda Babcock and Sara Laschever suggests that men are far more likely than women to negotiate their job offers (up to four times more likely).[66] The impact of not negotiating salaries can be very expensive for women over their lifetime earnings. We encourage you to be bold, confident, and creative in how and what you ask for, and secure more value in the offer. If needed, take a negotiations course, read books on the topic, and seek advice from your mentors and circle of influence.
- If you're in a position to hire and determine compensation packages, be more generous with women employees. Bump their salaries by 25 percent or more. We have decades of lost earnings to make up for!
- Become a volunteer leader and serve on committees and affinity groups within your workplace.
- Do research and challenge human resource benefits and policies that impact flexibly and support what working families need, including paid parental leave.
- Be an ally and educate yourself on matters related to DEIB (diversity, equity, inclusion, and belonging). Don't get sucked into the so-called culture wars. Read up on the motherhood

---

[66] Linda Babcock and Sara Laschever, *Ask for It: How Women Can Use the Power of Negotiation to Get What They Really Want:* (New York: Bantam, 2008), 4–14.

penalty and the fatherhood bonus[67] and how these and other sociological biases may be undercurrents in your workplace that are creating more barriers for women. Look under the rocks and bring light to the dark places in our organizational midst.

- ❋ Quote more women and cite women's work in your presentations, papers, and comments. Do the research and discover more women thought leaders. We recommend you follow Dana Rubin, author of *Speaking While Female*,[68] and download the free checklist from her consulting firm Speech Studio,[69] which helps organizations assess how well they're doing with developing the visibility and influence of their talented women.
- ❋ Hire women speakers for your conferences and pay them well. Did you know that to speak at an event, women are typically paid less than men (if they're paid at all)?

Stepping into Your Fearless Future

The Shero's Journey will present you with many opportunities and challenges, including celebrations and setbacks and plenty of wins and losses. Your quest to become a more fearless leader can begin today with a single step, a decision really: to choose to see yourself as the leader of your life, to step into your full brilliance and potential, and to make peace with your leadership shadow. To fear less and lead more.

If you still feel stuck and can't see an action to take, call us. We will help. If each one of us does something, anything, we will make a dent in the universe. We can each take one step closer to becoming a thriving, balanced, holistic leader rather than a one-dimensional leader. We

---

[67] Learn more about The Fatherhood Bonus at https://www.augsburg.edu/now/2017/11/16/the-fatherhood-bonus-and-the-motherhood-penalty//.
[68] Dana Rubin, *Speaking While Female: 75 Extraordinary Speeches by American Women* (New York: Real Clear Publishing, 2023).
[69] https://speech.studio/free-checklist/.

each have the power to create new opportunities and to expand women's voices and influence, starting with our own.

* * * * *

You will face many uncomfortable moments along your Shero's Journey, just as all the women whose stories we've shared did. We encourage you to keep going. Getting comfortable with the uncomfortable is the basis for all learning and growth. Embrace it all. Let your light shine through.

Fearlessly.

Fear less and LEAD MORE

Download the Book Club Discussion Kit.
Learn more about the women featured in this book.

Access bonus gifts here:
fearlessleaderbooks.com/bonuses

Appendix: Survey

In chapter 1, "Survey Says: Going Nowhere Fast," the authors refer to a survey that was conducted between November 2022 and February 2023. The survey was distributed through social media, mainly through LinkedIn and Facebook. Coauthor Kathy designed and deployed the survey, and coauthor Rosemary analyzed the results. The objective was to secure at least 100 responses, and they received a total of 122 submissions. Most responses were from women based in the United States. The authors' purpose in conducting this survey was to gather feedback and insights to inform their thinking and make this book more relevant to the current challenges faced by professional women who seek to advance their careers. This survey design and final size should not be considered a representative sample nor a reliable form of quantitative research. You can view the survey questions or take the survey yourself by scanning the QR code found on the next page.

Survey

Barriers to Leadership Advancement for Women

Take the survey and reflect on what's been holding you back from advancing in your career.

Get more information here:
fearlessleaderbooks.com/bonuses

Study Guide

This book was intended to get you thinking differently about yourself and your future. If you found yourself feeling a bit uncomfortable at times while reading this book, that's a good thing. Discomfort and disruption are necessary for growth. To help you continue along the growth path, we're providing this self-study guide. It contains questions to help you self-reflect and discover new insights about yourself. We've also developed a book club discussion guide if you want to read and discuss this book with a group of friends. You can access a free Book Club Kit that includes this discussion guide and other tips and ideas by scanning the QR code found at the end of chapter 10.

As you reflect on each of these study guide questions, ask yourself how it applies to your life. What one or two things could you do today that would begin your Shero's Journey? We encourage you to jot down notes below or journal your answers in a separate notebook.

1. What thoughts and feelings came up for you as you read the stories of the fearless female leaders featured in this book? What could you relate to? What aspects of their Shero's Journeys have you personally experienced?
2. What can you identify in their stories that could've helped these women succeed faster or reduce their suffering?
3. What do you see in these stories that could potentially help you succeed faster or reduce your struggles?

4. What unfair or unjust barriers have you faced? How could you begin to change your focus and redirect your energy so that you can overcome them and win?
5. What unconscious biases are you more self-aware of now that you've read these Shero's Journey stories?
6. If you could sit down with one of the fearless female leaders featured in this book and have a conversation, what questions would you like to ask? What are you curious about and what else do you want to know?
7. What could you do to help or mentor other women like Sylvia or Jane, Opal or Eva, Paula or Kim, or Jolly or Wendy who have faced and are still facing barriers to leadership? What elements did you notice in their Shero's Journeys that helped support them and kept them going?
8. What stands in your way of collaborating with others or asking for help to reach your goals?
9. When have you struggled with trying to live up to other people's expectations or trying to fit in? What would it take for you to break with tradition and carve your own path? What do you need to succeed?
10. When have you been blocked, excluded, or allowed yourself to be silenced by the Old Boys' Club? What advice would you give your younger self now that you've read these stories and reflected?
11. What would it take for you to trust yourself more and listen to your intuition? How might you benefit?
12. If you're a parent, how often do you find yourself prescribing the right path for your child to pursue? What could you do differently to empower and trust them to make their own life choices?
13. Which of these stories sheds more light on your purpose?
14. How has this book enhanced your life and leadership journey?
15. How will you pay it forward and empower other women and girls to become fearless female leaders?

More Fearless Resources

Recommended Programs

Coauthor Kathy McAfee's company, Kmc Brand Innovation, LLC, offers the following programs and services that may be of value to you during your Shero's Journey:

- **The Fearless Leader program** is an eight-week group mentoring experience designed to help you take your career and business to the next level. This cohort-based program is 100 percent virtual, global, and transformative. Working with your cohort peers and a skilled facilitator coach, you'll explore topics such as leadership mindset, communication, decision-making, and conflict resolution. Self-reflection, exercises, readings, and discussions will help increase your self-awareness, confidence, and leadership skills. Learn if this program is right for you or members of your team at www.TheFearlessLeader.com.
- **Fearless Accountability** is a mastermind group designed to help high achieving people set and meet goals more consistently. Empowering you with tools, habits, encouragement, and an accountability buddy each month, the group helps you build momentum and move in the direction of your dreams. Monthly virtual meetups and weekly check-ins give you the support you need to keep going. The team at Fearless Accountability will have your back and ensure that you stay on track. Enroll at www.FearlesssAccountability.com.

- **Other programs and services:**
    - Business coaching for women-owned and minority-owned small businesses
    - Presentation skills training workshops for employees of corporations
    - Speaker coaching and preparedness for high-stakes public speaking events
    - Virtual training seminars on topics of leadership, personal branding, and networking for DEIB affinity groups at organizations and associations
    - Coauthor book collaborations for thought leaders who want to build visibility, share knowledge and wisdom, and strengthen their platform by publishing a book in the Fearless Leader Books series. Learn more at www.FearlessLeaderBooks.com.

Coauthor Rosemary Paetow's company, Think inStrategy, offers the following programs and services:

- **Leader Labs** for executives and their management teams. These programs hone people's genius thinking and problem-solving skills by creating a strategic lens and a culture to manage more effectively.
- **Customized training** designed to support the growth of sustainable businesses of all shapes and sizes. Custom services include corporate retreats and summits, group workshops, and virtual seminars.
- **Individual coaching** to support leaders' growth and development in conflict resolution, driving results, and motivating quality performance in their staff.

Kathy and Rosemary have experienced and highly recommend the transformation training from these trusted professionals:

- **Actualized Leadership Training.** Get certified in the Actualized Performance Cycle with William L. Sparks and

Associates, LLC. This high-value immersive experience is outstanding for personal development as well as professional development for coaches, consultants, or talent development leaders looking to add to their menu of services. Dr. Sparks offers the training in a variety of formats, from a three-day, in-person training held at Queens University in Charlotte North Carolina to virtual facilitator training courses. Check out his website for the latest offerings: https://drwillsparks.com/training.

- **Vocal Awareness Institute**. Founded by Arthur Samuel Joseph, one of the world's foremost authorities on the human voice, the institute teaches communication mastery and empowerment through voice. In his books, blogs, and mastery-moment lessons, Joseph shares the wisdom and expertise he garnered over his sixty years of teaching. He offers individual speech coaching, live-led training seminars held all over the world, online self-paced courses, and mastermind groups. Studying with Joseph will transform not only your voice but your identity, sovereignty, and how you see yourself. Learn more at https://vocalawareness.com/.
- **What's Next? transition coaching program**. Facilitated by Wendy Green, certified coach and host of the *Hey, Boomer!* live show, this six-week coaching experience provides skilled guidance and support to help people who are transitioning into retirement find a more fulfilling life. Individual coaching and group workshops are offered. Learn more at https://hey-boomer.biz/coaching/.
- **The OpEd Project's Write to Change the World virtual workshop**. The OpEd organization's mission is to change who writes history. They accomplish this mission by scouting for and training under-represented experts (especially women) to take thought leadership positions in their fields (through op-eds and much more), connecting them with their international network of high-level media mentors and vetting and channeling the best new ideas and experts directly to media gatekeepers across all platforms. Their core workshop empowers and helps

you explore the source of your credibility, the patterns and elements of persuasion, the difference between being "right" and being effective, how to preach beyond the choir, and how to think bigger about what you know so that you can have more impact in the world. Learn more at https://www.theopedproject.org/workshops.
- **The Campaign School at Yale University (TCSYale)**. TCSYale is a nonpartisan, issue-neutral **campaign** training **program** that endeavors to increase the number and influence of **women** in elected and appointed offices in the United States and around the globe. This is excellent training for new candidates, seasoned politicians, campaign managers, and those wishing to amplify their voices in their communities. Learn more about how to run a campaign and the traditions around campaigning to win at https://www.tcsyale.org/.
- **PAX Programs**. Founded by Alison Armstrong, author, educator, and creator of the "Understanding Men" and "Understanding Women" transformational online series, the organization runs programs that empower women through understanding how men operate. Women learn to partner with both women and men in powerful, fulfilling ways. Learn more about their many workshops and offerings at https://www.alisonarmstrong.com/.

Our Favorite Books

In addition to the books listed in our bibliography and cited in the chapters, we wanted to share books that we just loved reading (and in some cases, books we loved writing) and recommend that you read too.

- *As A Woman: What I Learned about Power, Sex, and the Patriarchy after I Transitioned* by Paula Stone Williams
- *Ask For It: How Women Can Use the Power of Negotiation to Get What They Really Want* by Linda Babcock and Sara Laschever

MORE FEARLESS RESOURCES

- *Better. Bigger. Bolder: How to Break the Profit Barrier. Predictably.* by Rosemary Paetow and Bob Sher
- *Bittersweet: How Sorrow and Longing Make Us Whole* by Susan Cain
- *Defining YOU: How Smart Professionals Craft the Answers To: Who Are You? What Do You Do? How Can You Help Me?* by Mark LeBlanc, Kathy McAfee, and Henry DeVries
- *DEVELOP: 7 Practical Tools to Take Charge of Your Career* by Ted Fleming
- *Finding Me: A Memoir* by Viola Davis
- *GRIT: The Power of Passion and Perseverance* by Angela Duckworth
- *Inclusion Uncomplicated: A Transformative Guide to Simplify DEI* by Dr. Nika White
- *Juneteenth: A Children's Story* by Opal Lee
- *Kitchen Table Wisdom: Stories That Heal* by Rachel Naomi Remen
- *Mad Honey: A Novel* by Jodi Picoult and Jennifer Finney Boylan
- *Networking Ahead: Get Where You Want to Go by Making Powerful, Professional Connections* by Kathy McAfee
- *Sharpening Your Point: Winning the Battle for Communication* by Leesa Wallace and Kathy McAfee
- *Staying in the Thriver Zone: A Road Map to Manifest a Life of Power and Purpose* by Susan M. Omilian
- *Stop Global Boring: How to Create Engaging Presentations that Motivate Audiences to Action* by Kathy McAfee
- *The Dark Side of the Light Chasers: Reclaiming Your Power, Creativity, Brilliance, and Dreams* by Debbie Ford
- *The Heroine's Journey: A Woman's Quest for Wholeness* (30th anniversary edition) by Maureen Murdoch
- *The Most Powerful You: 7 Bravery-Boosting Paths to Career Bliss* by Kathy Caprino
- *The Right Questions: Ten Essential Questions to Guide You to an Extraordinary Life* by Debbie Ford
- *Transitions: Making Sense of Life's Changes* (40th anniversary edition) by William Bridges and Susan Bridges

- *TRIPPING From Cleveland to Paris & Beyond* by Hermine Fuerst
- *Use Your Difference to Make a Difference: How to Connect and Communicate in a Cross-Cultural World* by Tayo Rockson
- *Vocal Leadership: 7 Minutes a Day to Communication Mastery* by Arthur Samuel Joseph
- *Women and Leadership: Real Lives, Real Lessons* by Julia Gillard and Ngozi Okonjo-Iweala

Movies

- *Barbie* (2023)
- *Everything, Everywhere, All at Once* (2023)
- *The Woman King* (2022)
- *Encanto* (2021)
- *Black Panther* (2018)
- *Wonder Woman* (2017)
- *Moana* (2016)
- *Hidden Figures* (2016)
- *Frida* (2002)
- *Ever After* (1998)

Speeches

A must-have resource for any fearless female leader is the Speaking While Female Speech Bank, which was developed by Dana Rubin and is now one of the largest repositories of female speeches throughout history (organized by topic and category). In her book by the same title, Rubin also provides biographical information and context about these fearless female leaders. If you need a reminder of the power and importance of women and their words, we recommend buying and reading her book as well as bookmarking her website and visiting it regularly: https://speakingwhilefemale.co/.

Podcasts

You can subscribe and listen to these recommended podcasts on your favorite podcast app or anywhere you find podcasts (Spotify, Apple, CastBox, Castnet, etc.):

- *Girl Take the Lead* with host Yolanda (Yo) Canny (https://girltaketheleadpod.com)
- *Hey, Boomer!* with host Wendy Green (https://heyboomer.biz/)
- *Relationships Rule* with host Janice Porter (https://www.janiceporter.com/podcast.html)
- *SAYge Real Stories* with host Linda Nedell (https://blog.saygelink.com/category/media)
- *The Moth: Storytelling Hour* (https://themoth.org/podcast)
- *The Rachel Maddow Show* (https://the-rachel-maddow-show.simplecast.com)
- *Velshi Banned Book Club* (hosted by MSNBC and Peacock TV)

Organizations

- Guiding Light for Orphans, Inc. (https://www.guidinglightorphans.org/)
- Mothers' Day Movement (http://www.mothersdaymovement.org/)
- Ms. Foundation for Women (https://forwomen.org/)
- PFLAG Association (https://pflag.org/)
- The Geena Davis Institute on Gender in Media (https://seejane.org/about-us/)
- Untapped Potential Inc. (https://www.upotential.org/)

Bibliography

"S.475 - Juneteenth National Independence Day Act." Congress.gov. Last modified June 17, 2021. https://www.congress.gov/bill/117th-congress/senate-bill/475/text.

Al-Mondhiry, Jafar, Margot Hedlin, Katie Watson, Samuel Shem, and Tamar Schiff. "Gallows Humor." Produced by Core IM. *At the Bedside*. October 30, 2019. Podcast, MP3 audio, 47:04. https://www.coreimpodcast.com/2019/10/30/gallows-humor/.

American Association of University Women. "The Motherhood Penalty." Accessed October 4, 2023. https://www.aauw.org/issues/equity/motherhood/.

Babcock, Linda, and Sara Laschever. *Ask For It: How Women Can Use the Power of Negotiation to Get What They Really Want*. New York: Bantam, 2008.

Bahadur, Nina. "6 Women Who Credit Their Male Mentors with Helping Them Find Success." HuffPost. Last modified December 6, 2017. https://www.huffpost.com/entry/women-mentored-by-men-gender-matter_n_3894659.

Ball, Aimee Lee. "Women and the Negativity Receptor." Oprah.com. Accessed August 17, 2023. https://www.oprah.com/omagazine/why-women-have-low-self-esteem-how-to-feel-more-confident/all.

Balnicke, Janelle, and David Kennard, dir. *The Hero's Journey: The World of Joseph Campbell*. 1987; Hudson, OH: Acorn Media, 2012. DVD.

Barger, Amira. "What Society Gets Wrong About the 'Angry Black Woman' Stereotype." MSNBC. April 17, 2023. https://www.msnbc.com/know-your-value/business-culture/what-society-gets-wrong-about-angry-black-woman-stereotype-n1304353.

Brizendine, Louann. *The Female Brain*. New York: Harmony Books, 2007.

Brizendine, Louann. *The Male Brain: A Breakthrough Understanding of How Men and Boys Think*. New York: Harmony Books, 2011.

Buchholz, Katharina. "How Has the Number of Female CEOs in Fortune 500 Companies Changed over the Last 20 Years?" World Economic Forum. March 10, 2022. https://www.weforum.org/agenda/2022/03/ceos-fortune-500-companies-female.

Budig, Michelle J. "The Fatherhood Bonus and The Motherhood Penalty: Parenthood and the Gender Gap in Pay." Third Way. September 2, 2014. https://www.thirdway.org/report/the-fatherhood-bonus-and-the-motherhood-penalty-parenthood-and-the-gender-gap-in-pay.

Cain, Susan. *Bittersweet: How Sorrow and Longing Make Us Whole*. New York: Crown, 2023.

Campbell, Joseph. *The Hero with a Thousand Faces*. New Jersey: Princeton University Press, 2004.

"Women CEO's in America" 2022 Annual Report by Women Business Collaborative (WBC), with Ascend, C200 and Catalyst. https://wbcollaborative.org/women-ceo-report/the-report/2023-executive-summary/.

Coutu, Diane. "How Resilience Works." Harvard Business Review. May 2002. https://hbr.org/2002/05/how-resilience-works.

Daly, Michael J. "The Story of Harry's Remarkable Mother." CTPost. May 8, 2016. https://www.ctpost.com/news/article/The-story-of-Harry-s-remarkable-mother-7421563.php.

BIBLIOGRAPHY

Diamond, Rachel. "The Motherhood Penalty in the Workplace." Psychology Today. February 13, 2023. https://www.psychologytoday.com/us/blog/preparing-for-parenthood/202302/the-motherhood-penalty-in-the-workplace#:~:text.

Ellis, Chris. "The Pillars of Leadership Wisdom." University of Chicago | Center for Practical Wisdom. July 6, 2020. https://wisdomcenter.uchicago.edu/news/discussions/pillars-leadership-wisdom.

Epps, Peter G. "10 Greatest Poems Written by John Milton." Society of Classical Poets. November 7, 2017. https://classicalpoets.org/2017/11/07/10-greatest-poems-written-by-john-milton/.

Federal Trade Commission. "Equal Credit Opportunity Act." Accessed October 4, 2023. https://www.ftc.gov/legal-library/browse/statutes/equal-credit-opportunity-act.

Fry, Richard. "U.S. Women Near Milestone in the College-Educated Labor Force." Pew Research Center. June 20, 2019. https://www.pewresearch.org/short-reads/2019/06/20/u-s-women-near-milestone-in-the-college-educated-labor-force/.

Gaston, Peter. "Exclusive: Margaret Cho Teams with Tegan & Sara!" SPIN. August 2, 2010. https://www.spin.com/2010/08/exclusive-margaret-cho-teams-tegan-sara/.

Gladwell, Malcolm. *The Tipping Point: How Little Things Can Make a Big Difference*. New York: Back Bay Books, 2002.

Goleman, Daniel, Richard Boyatzis, and Annie McKee. *Primal Leadership: Realizing the Power of Emotional Intelligence*. Boston: Harvard Business School Press, 2002.

Johnson, Marty, and Alex Gangitano. "Biden Signs Juneteenth Bill: 'Great Nations Don't Ignore Their Most Painful Moments.'" The Hill. June 17, 2021. https://thehill.com/homenews/administration/559057-biden-signs-juneteenth-bill-great-nations-dont-ignore-their-most/.

Joseph, Arthur Samuel. *Vocal Leadership: 7 Minutes a Day to Communication Mastery*. New York: McGraw Hill, 2014.

Kagan, Julia. "Glass Cliff: Definition, Research, Examples, vs. Glass Ceiling." Investopedia. Last modified December 7, 2022. https://www.investopedia.com/terms/g/glass-cliff.asp#.

Kochhar, Rakesh. "The Enduring Grip of the Gender Pay Gap." Pew Research Center. March 1, 2023. https://www.pewresearch.org/social-trends/2023/03/01/the-enduring-grip-of-the-gender-pay-gap/.

Kristof, Nicholas D., and Sheryl WuDunn. *Half the Sky: Turning Oppression into Opportunity for Women Worldwide*. New York: Vintage Books, 2010.

Kristof, Nickolas. "Celebrate: Save a Mother." *New York Times*. May 8, 2010. https://www.nytimes.com/2010/05/09/opinion/09kristof.html?searchResultPosition=1.

LeBlanc, Mark, Kathy McAfee, and Henry DeVries. *Defining YOU: How Smart Professionals Craft the Answers To: Who Are You? What Do You Do? How Can You Help Me?* Oceanside, CA: Indie Books International, 2018.

Mariechild, Diane. *The Inner Dance: A Guide to Spiritual and Psychological Unfolding*. Freedom, CA: Crossing Press, 1987.

Marshall, Penny, dir. *A League of Their Own*. 1992; Culver City, CA: Columbia Pictures, 2004. DVD.

Murdock, Maureen. *The Heroine's Journey: Woman's Quest for Wholeness*. Boulder, CO: Shambhala, 2020.

National Archives. "The Emancipation Proclamation." Last modified January 28, 2022. https://www.archives.gov/exhibits/featured-documents/emancipation-proclamation?_ga=2.101893444.494502383.1684326284-213107575.1683210851.

National Archives. "War Department General Order 143: Creation of the U.S. Colored Troops (1863)." Milestone Documents. Accessed August 9, 2023. https://www.archives.gov/milestone-documents/war-department-general-order-143.

BIBLIOGRAPHY

NobelPrize.org. "The Sveriges Riksbank Prize in Economic Sciences in Memory of Alfred Nobel 2023." Accessed November 30, 2023. https://www.nobelprize.org/prizes/economic-sciences/2023/popular-information/.

Noland, Marcus, and Tyler Moran. "Study: Firms with More Women in the C-Suite Are More Profitable." Peterson Institute for International Economics. February 8, 2016. https://www.piie.com/commentary/op-eds/study-firms-more-women-c-suite-are-more-profitable.

O'Brien, David. "The Values Clarity Worksheet." WorkChoice Solutions. Accessed August 9, 2023. http://www.workchoicesolutions.com/images/The_Values_Clarity_Worksheet.pdf.

Opal's Walk 2 DC. "The Real Opal Lee." Accessed August 9, 2023. https://www.opalswalk2dc.com/about#.

PFLAG. "About Us." Accessed August 9, 2023. https://pflag.org/about-us/.

Pincus, Randi. "Anti-Defamation League's 2011 Daniel R. Ginsberg Humanitarian Award Reception." Patch. October 19, 2011. https://patch.com/connecticut/greenwich/an--anti-defamation-leagues-2011-daniel-r-ginsberg-hu429bdd2e7d.

Post, Corinne, and Chris Byron. "Women on Boards and Firm Financial Performance: A Meta-Analysis." *Academy of Management Journal* 58, no. 5 (October 2015). https://journals.aom.org/doi/10.5465/amj.2013.0319.

Rubin, Dana. *Speaking While Female: 75 Extraordinary Speeches by American Women*. New York: Real Clear Publishing, 2023.

Saska, Jim. "Juneteenth Is Now a Federal Holiday, as Biden Signs Bill." Roll Call. June 17, 2021. https://rollcall.com/2021/06/17/juneteenth-is-now-a-federal-holiday-as-biden-signs-bill/.

Sparks, William L. *Actualized Leadership: Meeting Your Shadow & Maximizing Your Potential*. Alexandria, VA: Society for Human Resource Management Press, 2019.

Surillo, Samantha. "Successful Mentor Programs: Demystifying the Key Benefits & Elements." Courtex Performance. November 2022. https://www.courtexperformance.com/whitepaper.

Truman Library Institute. "Truman Quotes." Accessed September 15, 2023. https://www.trumanlibraryinstitute.org/truman/truman-quotes/.

Tulshyan, Ruchika, and Jodi-Ann Burey. "Stop Telling Women They Have Imposter Syndrome." Harvard Business Review. February 22, 2021. https://hbr.org/2021/02/stop-telling-women-they-have-imposter-syndrome.

U.S. Bureau of Labor Statistics. "Labor Force Statistics from the Current Population Survey." Accessed October 4, 2023. https://www.bls.gov/cps/aa2019/cpsaat10.htm.

Victor, Daniel. "Women in Company Leadership Tied to Stronger Profits, Study Says." *New York Times*. February 9, 2016. https://www.nytimes.com/2016/02/10/business/women-in-company-leadership-tied-to-stronger-profits.html.

Wallis, Jay. "Members of Congress Nominate Texas' Opal Lee for Nobel Peace Prize." WFAA-TV. Last modified August 18, 2023. https://www.wfaa.com/article/news/local/opal-lee-nominated-nobel-peace-prize/287-924dfd36-69ff-4b4a-84d3-4b10214883dd.

Wezerek, Gus, and Kristen R. Ghodsee. "Women's Unpaid Labor is Worth $10,900,000,000." *New York Times*. March 5, 2020. https://www.nytimes.com/interactive/2020/03/04/opinion/women-unpaid-labor.html.

Williams, Paula Stone. *As a Woman: What I Learned about Power, Sex, and the Patriarchy after I Transitioned*. New York: Atria Books, 2021.

Acknowledgments

Writing a book, like raising a child, takes a village. We are deeply grateful for everyone who inspired, supported, and carried us over the finish line on this ambitious book project. If we've left off your name here, please forgive us. Please know that your contribution to our thinking and writing, as well as the role you played in our Shero's Journeys, made a difference.

To our mission-aligned publishing partners, the talented team at Publish Your Purpose, including CEO and owner Jenn T. Grace, project manager extraordinaire Alexander Loutsenko, operations director Niki Gallagher-Garcia, all things money Cari Dawson, insightful editor Nancy Graham-Tillman (who provided the most thorough, high-value editorial review these authors have ever received), proofreader Lily Capstick and the talented cover designer Julia Kuris. Thank you all for your tremendous contributions and faith in us.

To our creative team at Peculiar Agency, Amy Pecoraro and Jon McConnell. Thank you for bringing your brilliance to our book project, brand, and website.

To the eight fearless women whose stories appear in this book and the many others who sat for an interview and shared their stories and Glimpses. We are deeply humbled and honored to know you. Your Shero's Journeys remain etched in our hearts and minds. Thank you for trusting us and allowing us to walk in your shoes, if only for a short while. You are truly our Sheroes.

To all the many graduates of The Fearless Leader program, especially Megan L. Robinson, Amanda Dumas, Toni Sprouse, and Wendy

Green, who contributed to this book and influenced our thinking in profound ways.

To Teresa C. Younger, president and CEO of Ms. Foundation for Women. Thank you for your unrelenting leadership and fearless advocacy for women and girls everywhere.

To the wonderful people who completed our survey and shared with us the barriers they've faced in pursuing leadership advancement. Some of you chose to remain anonymous, and we honor that and thank you. Others agreed to be listed in our book. Here they are, fearless in their own right:

*Kathleen Adams * Michelle Andersen * Nancy Anton * Shameka Argo * Michelle Fenton Begley * Laura Bobe * Gretel Bolaños * Karyn Buxman * Lena Calvo-Blake * Eileen Candels * Yolanda Canny * Patricia Celentano * Rachel Chapman * Kath Cooper * Kathleen D'Andraia * Jeannette Dardenne * Monica De La Torre * Lorna Diane * Violeta Diaz * Dorra Djebbi-Simmons * Amy Dunn * Kay Etherington * Angela Balfour Franklin * Jennifer Frederick * Sheryne Glicksman * Tammi Hart * Birgit Heidorn * Claire Hintz * Miriam Hyman * Yoellie Iglesias * Michelle Jones * Sarah King * Myra Lee * Lorena Llaguno * Gabrielle Mack * Laurie Malecki * Kim McKeage * Tiffany Mclallen * Rose Mihaly * Roxanna Booth Miller * Tianna Miller * Helene Morris * Peggy Moulton * Andrea Myers * Kelly Nygren * Mary O'Meara * Chi Chi Okezie * Nija Orr * Michelle Ozumba * Tiffany Palacio-Barrales * Judy Peabody * Deborah Peterson * Deborah Petrelle * Nona Prather * Clare Price * Deborah Randolph Price * Asha Rani * Cindi Rosner * Nancy Schumann * Gennie Siwicki * Cindy Spaans * Beth Sprole * Shannon Strickland * Karla Sustaita * Kate Sutch * Tracy Symolon * Kelly Tantraporn * Tracy Thompson * Ida Thomsen * Rita Tustin * Lindsay Valenzuela * Cristal Velez * Faye Williamson * Bethany Winston * Desiree Wolfe * and Donna Wotton.*

To Henry DeVries for playing the role of matchmaker and first suggesting we cowrite a leadership book. There's nothing like having a strong accountability partner to push you out of writer's block.

* * * * *

ACKNOWLEDGMENTS

Coauthor Rosemary would like to especially thank the following people in her life:

To Kathy McAfee, a constant inspiration for what's possible when working together to create something bigger, better. Your love and appreciation are so empowering.

To my husband, Rahul Singh, who sees me bigger than I see myself and constantly demands that I stop hiding my gifts and talents. Thank you for always having my back.

To my son, Christopher Paetow, who has taken what he has learned from his parents and become a wise, thoughtful, and creative man. Love you to the moon and back—always.

To my parents, Herbert and Maria von Hammerstein, who first taught me how to think strategically, how to visualize, how to be a leader, and how to love unconditionally. Between the tennis, the cooking, and the managing of my little brother at out-of-town tennis tournaments, I learned to trust myself and get creative around problems. I wish everyone could've been taught by you two.

To my little brother, Charles, who taught me kindness, patience, and teamwork. I couldn't ask for a better coconspirator than you.

To all my clients who continually challenge me to be better, and who inspire me with their courage and commitment to being their best selves regardless of what shows up.

To my other coauthor Bob Sher, who is such a great support and a genius around presenting materials.

To all my friends who love me unconditionally. Thank you for having my back.

* * * * *

Coauthor Kathy would like to especially thank the following fearless and fabulous people in her life:

To Rosemary Paetow. Thank you for being my writing partner. I greatly enjoyed our weekly Monday writeup sessions. You taught me so much and listened so well.

To my husband, Byron Schoenholzer. Thank you for being the best, most supportive, and patient partner I could ever have wished for. You have been by my side for five books now, with many more in the works.

To my parents, Roz and Chuck McAfee, for inspiring my love of dancing, writing, and speaking my mind—all important building blocks of leadership.

To my brother, Rod McAfee, for your technical brilliance and endless generosity.

To Samantha (Sam) McCracken and Rachel Pellegrini, my fearless virtual assistants from Sharp Business Support. Thank you for being on my success team. I couldn't have created this wonderful work without your expertise and unwavering support!

To my Aunt Hermine, who has served many roles in my life including mentor, friend, and editor. Your words of wisdom continue to ring in my heart.

To Adrienne Milics, my dear friend, colleague, and mentor. I can always turn to you for perspective and sage advice. Thank you for contributing to this book by proposing the winning subtitle.

To Dr. William Sparks and his team at Queens University at University of Charlotte, including the invincible Jane Williams, the brilliant Erika Weed, and the ever-curious Jon (JC) Fedorczyk. Thank you for enriching my life and deepening my understanding of self-actualization and resilience.

To Rachel Maddow, the fearless MSNBC news host and political commentator, author, historical storyteller, and change agent. It's because of you that I first learned of Ms. Opal Lee and sought her out for an interview.

To the healthcare professionals and other essential workers who fearlessly showed up every day for work during the COVID-19 global pandemic. Your emotional courage gave me the courage and confidence to branch out and do something different and bolder. You inspired me to create The Fearless Leader™ program.

To George Floyd, Breonna Taylor, Ahmaud Arbery, and all those who continue to face racism and discrimination. Your unjust suffering awakened something powerful in me. You gave me the

ACKNOWLEDGMENTS

courage to acknowledge my own White privilege and to merge my personal and professional goals in pursuit of social and racial justice.

* * * * *

And finally, to you dear reader. We thank you for continuing to believe in the role that books play in our learning, growth and leadership development. Keep reading!

About the Authors

Kathy McAfee is an accomplished author and speaker, creative entrepreneur, and business coach. She thrives on helping professionals advance their careers and influence and partners with organizations and communities to cultivate leadership diversity. Known as America's Marketing Motivator, Kathy is the founder of The Fearless Leader program and Fearless Leader Books series.

A graduate of Stanford University in economics, Kathy spent more than twenty years in Corporate America with companies such as Levi Strauss, Maybelline, and Southcorp Wines of Australia, where she developed a passion and expertise for marketing and branding. In 2005, she launched her own business, an adventure she recommends to anyone with a spirit of adventure and the stomach for uncertainty.

Kathy is a Master Practitioner of Neuro Linguistic Programming (NLP) and a certified professional in Actualized Performance. She is qualified to provide assessments and training in Actualized Leader Profile, ALP 360°, and Actualized Team Profile.

In 2015, Kathy got the idea that she might want to run for public office someday soon, so she attended a weeklong intensive training program at The Campaign School at Yale University.

But perhaps the most fun and freedom Kathy has enjoyed in her long career is owning and operating Kmc Brand Innovation, LLC, a talent development and empowerment company offering coaching, training, motivation, and accountability to emerging leaders of all kinds.

Kathy has authored and coauthored several business books, including *Stop Global Boring*, *Networking Ahead*, *Sharpening Your Point* with Leesa Wallace, *Defining YOU* with Mark LeBlanc and Henry DeVries, and *Fearless Female Leaders* with Rosemary Paetow. She's a true believer in the power of collaboration and connection to make the world a better place, and she has big plans for the nonfiction book series Fearless Leader Books ™.

For health and happiness, Kathy enjoys gardening, walking, and hula hooping (the latter for which she claims to have won a few competitions, but no documentation can be found). She has recently taken to pickleball where she has earned the nickname "Corner Kathy." She's also a student of Taekwondo, in which she and her husband Byron have earned a second- and third-degree black belt, respectively.

As an ovarian cancer survivor, Kathy will gladly share her story and lend a supportive ear to anyone going through that journey. She's committed to paying it forward. She can be reached at Kathy@TheFearlessLeader.com

Connect with Kathy on social media:
- LinkedIn: https://www.linkedin.com/in/kathymcafee/
- Facebook: https://www.facebook.com/KathyMcAfeeMarketingMotivator/
- Instagram: @kathymcafeemarketingmotivator
- Website: https://thefearlessleader.com
- YouTube Channels: https://www.youtube.com/@thefearlessleader and https://www.youtube.com/kathymcafee

ABOUT THE AUTHORS

Rosemary Paetow, CEO of Think inStrategy, combines a rare talent in logical skills (financial, strategic, and systems thinking) with the soft skills of emotional intelligence and self-awareness to develop better, bolder leaders. She first developed an eye for talent and leadership potential as a tennis instructor before taking that insight into the business world and learning from the bottom up how to manage a team to excel at the highest levels.

Attaining her CPA at KPMG, one of the top four accounting firms in the world, she learned to quickly identify a company's key business risks and refined her systemic thinking. She then ventured out to build her own enterprise where she could empower more CEOs to lead and inspire their teams to perform at world-class levels. Comfortable among industry giants, Rosemary successfully served as a Vistage Chair, leading peer-to-peer CEO groups for nine years. She now runs a successful consulting practice where she helps business owners meet and exceed their goals.

An avid reader and knowledge seeker, Rosemary pivoted from her degree in biochemistry to expand her interest and expertise to human chemistry and business acceleration. She's committed to personal development and lifelong learning.

With this powerful combination of skills, experience, and curiosity, Rosemary now serves as a mentor and coach with The Fearless Leader program.

Rosemary has coauthored several books, including *Better. Bigger. Bolder. How to Break the Profit Barrier. Predictably.* with Bob Sher and *Fearless Female Leaders* with Kathy McAfee.

As a breast cancer survivor and uterine cancer survivor, Rosemary will gladly share her journey and lend a supportive ear to anyone going through a similar process. She's committed to paying it forward. She can be reached at rpaetow@thinknstrategy.com.

Connect with Rosemary on social media:
- LinkedIn: https://www.linkedin.com/in/rosemarypaetow/
- Facebook: https://www.facebook.com/rosemary.paetow/
- Website: https://thinkinstrategy.com/about-us

The B Corp Movement

Dear reader,

Thank you for reading this book and joining the Publish Your Purpose community! You are joining a special group of people who aim to make the world a better place.

What's Publish Your Purpose About?

Our mission is to elevate the voices often excluded from traditional publishing. We intentionally seek out authors and storytellers with diverse backgrounds, life experiences, and unique perspectives to publish books that will make an impact in the world.

Beyond our books, we are focused on tangible, action-based change. As a woman- and LGBTQ+-owned company, we are committed to reducing inequality, lowering levels of poverty, creating a healthier environment, building stronger communities, and creating high-quality jobs with dignity and purpose.

As a Certified B Corporation, we use business as a force for good. We join a community of mission-driven companies building a more equitable, inclusive, and sustainable global economy. B Corporations must meet high standards of transparency, social and environmental performance, and accountability as determined by the nonprofit B Lab. The certification process is rigorous and ongoing (with a recertification requirement every three years).

How Do We Do This?

We intentionally partner with socially and economically disadvantaged businesses that meet our sustainability goals. We embrace and encourage our authors and employee's differences in race, age, color, disability, ethnicity, family or marital status, gender identity or expression, language, national origin, physical and mental ability, political affiliation, religion, sexual orientation, socio-economic status, veteran status, and other characteristics that make them unique.

Community is at the heart of everything we do—from our writing and publishing programs to contributing to social enterprise nonprofits like reSET (https://www.resetco.org/) and our work in founding B Local Connecticut.

We are endlessly grateful to our authors, readers, and local community for being the driving force behind the equitable and sustainable world we are building together.

To connect with us online, or publish with us, visit us at www.publishyourpurpose.com.

Elevating Your Voice,

Jenn T. Grace

Jenn T. Grace
Founder, Publish Your Purpose

Begin Your Shero's Journey Now!

THE Fearless LEADER™

Apply Now
TheFearlessLeader.com

Printed in the USA
CPSIA information can be obtained
at www.ICGtesting.com
LVHW091928200624
783444LV00006B/26/J

9 798887 970943